DEBT REDUCTION

WITH TOM COPLAND
(Chartered Professional Accountant)

*Biblical Principles to Deal With
Inflation, High Interest Rates,
and Eliminating Debt*

Debt Reduction with Tom Copland
Copyright ©2022 Tom Copland

Published by Castle Quay Books
Burlington, Ontario, Canada and Jupiter, Florida, U.S.A.
416-573-3249 | info@castlequaybooks.com | www.castlequaybooks.com

Edited by Julie Child
Cover design and book interior by Burst Impressions

978-1-988928-71-5 Soft Cover
978-1-988928-72-2 E-book

Library and Archives Canada Cataloguing in Publication

Title: Debt reduction : biblical principles to deal with inflation, high interest rates and eliminating debt / by Tom Copland.
Names: Copland, Tom, 1953- author.
Identifiers: Canadiana 20220256993 | ISBN 9781988928715 (softcover)
Subjects: LCSH: Finance, Personal—Religious aspects—Christianity. | LCSH: Christians—Finance, Personal. | LCSH: Debt.
Classification: LCC HG179 .C67 2022 | DDC 332.024/02—dc23

CASTLE QUAY BOOKS

The headline in today's *Financial Post* reads: "Bank of Canada raises interest rate." In its official statement, the Bank of Canada said, "The Bank will use its monetary policy tools to return inflation to target." That's fancy talk for "the interest rates are going up...fast." There was a time when this headline would have induced stress and panic in me. Twelve years ago, my debt was in excess of $500,000. With three children attending American universities, the path to debt freedom was not clear. Gratefully, that's when I met Tom Copland. He taught me the principles you are about to learn and encouraged me to aim for complete debt freedom. My current debt is less than $5,000, and I am only months away from having no debt of any kind! Friend, financial peace is within your grasp. Please read this book carefully and apply it relentlessly. The book you now hold is the vehicle you need for your financial journey!

Reverend Don Symons, senior pastor at Westney Heights Baptist Church, Ajax, Ontario, Canada; former executive with a large multinational technology company

If you are looking for an excuse to stay in debt, *do not* read this book! Tom is a man of detail and has removed every excuse for remaining in debt, while providing many practical ways to get out of debt.

Reverend Jack Hannah, retired pastor and current ministry leader at Westney Heights Baptist Church, Ajax, Ontario, Canada

Tom's heart and passion for helping people manage money and achieve financial freedom are unmatched by anyone I've ever met. An example of this is his book on debt reduction. *Debt Reduction* is timeless and a must-read for everyone, regardless of whether one is struggling with debt or already debt-free. The wisdom, biblical teaching, and practical instructions presented in his book are the entire package on how to get out of debt and never go back! It is one of the most straightforward books to read and understand about financial management out there. Every page is filled with knowledge and topics crucial to achieving and maintaining financial freedom.

Randy Ziegenhagel, Financial Coach and Culture Development Advisor, former Global Culture Officer and V.P. of Business Development and Electronic Manufacturing Industry

TESTIMONIES

Reading Tom's book was like having him in the room teaching me all over again. What a benefit for those who do not have the time to participate in a weekly study! Tom's practice of using Scripture to support timeless biblical financial principles is what equips people to understand God's way of managing finances, allowing them to grow closer to God in their financial journey. With expanded topics and case studies, it is an asset even for those who have completed Tom's original small group study.

Liisa Snell, Financial Coach and small group leader of Financial Management God's Way

Tom's teaching on debt reduction is very countercultural as it implores the reader to begin to understand God's perspective on debt and how this compares to a typical worldly, non-biblical view on borrowing and debt accumulation. Tom's book provides extensive Bible study resources on this topic. It highlights certain key areas, such as contentment, for its readers to focus on, which has been critical for my personal financial journey.

The book is valuable for Christians desiring to learn the necessary biblical financial principles to eliminate their debt. It provides excellent practical examples of the significant differ-ence in interest costs incurred by those who borrow versus those who save. And to help avoid such unnecessary burdens of debt, Tom prioritizes a particular emphasis on developing and implementing a budget as a financial planning tool that could benefit all who utilize it.

Tom Copland's book is quite timely given our North American society's general tendency to borrow to fund various expenditures, regardless of affordability. The book provides insightful biblical and practical wisdom that can help anyone trying to prepare for and mitigate the potential consequences of significant interest costs related to debt accumulation over the next several years.

I have been involved with Copland Financial Ministries as a small group leader, seminar leader, and financial coach, since 2011. I have witnessed the impact that learning and implementing this material has had on those who have taken this course, along with my own life.

I highly encourage anyone to spend the time to thoroughly review the material within this book, which is not typically taught in churches. If you do, and you allow it to replace any worldly attitudes towards money and material things, I am highly confident you will enjoy God's blessings far into the future.

Eli Papakirykos, Chartered Financial Analyst

Tom offers a practical and biblically based approach for dealing with debt. If you are in debt or just want to better manage your finances, this book is an invaluable resource. This book also complements Tom's radio and television ministry by providing additional details and helpful case studies.

Dan Tomlinson, MBA, B.A.Sc. Engineering, Financial Coach and small group leader of Financial Management God's Way

I was able to start reading your book, *Debt Reduction, Biblical Principles to Deal with Inflation, Higher Interest and Eliminating Debt.* I'm barely into it and already sense God's presence as I read! Tom, I truly love you, brother. You are such an encouragement to so many people and me. The way you include Scripture throughout your writing is timely and applicable. You have the gift of teaching the Bible so clearly and effectively. Most certainly, God has hand-picked you for this ministry, and I'm sure thankful for that! God bless you, Tom!

R.Z., Holland Landing, Ontario, Canada

I'm reading through this book by Tom Copland. Wow, is it good! And wow, did I break so many of God's financial principles! I admit I made some terrible decisions, but I will learn from them and not make the same errors in the future. There are many valuable lessons to take from this! God has changed me in the process and saved me from greater disaster.

Adam, Ontario, Canada

The workshop series was highly educational in practical finance and anchored in Scripture. I learned as much, or even more, about Scripture as I did financial principles. Tom's knowledge of the Bible is extraordinary, and God's call on his life is unmistakable, allowing so many people the opportunity to learn and understand how to manage their finances God's way. Tom's generosity in offering this program without charging a fee is a testament to his commitment to God and people. It is evident that Tom lives out his faith and demonstrates his faithfulness to love God and others.

W.B., Barrie, Ontario, Canada

Tom, your biblical advice has made a huge difference in our finances over the past couple of years. Thanks again.

L.T., Oxbow, Saskatchewan, Canada

Tom, I attended one of your courses years ago, and your humbleness before the Lord and teachings have stayed with me. Praise God, I am debt free and able to use my knowledge of biblical financial principles to help others. Many thanks for your ministry.

L.P., Toronto, Ontario, Canada

Thank you, Tom, for your teaching session and personal testimony, which were very helpful! I needed to hear many of the things you taught and discussed. You are a great example of faithfulness to the Lord.

R.S., Prince George, British Columbia, Canada

Thank you, Tom, for leading our finance course! It has helped convict my heart to make some practical changes. The difference between this course and another course my wife and I took years ago is the infusion of God's word in the curriculum. It's neat having my Bible beside me while I'm working through the case studies. Thank you for providing such a strong biblical foundation to what we are learning. Not only is my pocketbook being challenged, but my heart is as well. God is also challenging my thinking on faith and deepening my trust in Him.

T.N., Calgary, Alberta, Canada

My knowledge and understanding of God's financial principles has profoundly changed. The Bible is a wealth of information on how we should wisely think about and manage our finances. I wish I had learned these principles sooner.

L.G., Toronto, Ontario, Canada

I am excited that your financial ministry is changing people's lives all over the world! Taking your course helped me develop a new money mindset and broke a stronghold in my life. I am still learning to walk in God's ways of managing finances, but I have come a long way! In the future, I would like to take part in a financial coaching webinar to learn how to help others.

J.C., Waterloo, Ontario, Canada

Thank you, Tom, for teaching God's word faithfully, and for the many hours you spend of your own time for our benefit and to answer God's call. It has been a life-changing experience, which I very much appreciate. As a thank you, I am sending a donation to your ministry today, and I will continue to pray for your ministry too. Thank you again for all you do.

L.M., Stouffville, Ontario, Canada

Tom, I took your Financial Management God's Way course last fall, and thanks to your biblical advice and God's leading and guidance, I have paid off my mortgage!

B.C., Ontario, Canada

I sincerely thank Tom and Copland Financial Ministries for hosting these wonderful sessions on Financial Management God's Way. The teachings motivated me to pay off my mortgage sooner than later, and I'm forever grateful! Thank you, Tom, for taking the time to chat with me after our session. I value your insights, along with the tips you gave me. Praise the Lord who enabled me to pay off my mortgage! I'm so glad I'm mortgage-free!

S.P., Toronto, Ontario, Canada

I write you with a heart of praise and thanksgiving to God as I paid off a $5,000 creditor account today! Glory to God! Truly the Lord has been merciful toward me and helped me so much. Your ministry has been a tremendous blessing, and your financial advice helped me avoid taking on a loan with a 40 per cent interest rate just to pay off another debt. I cannot thank you enough and those who labor with you in your ministry.

N.F., Brampton, Ontario, Canada

I attended the financial workshop and by God's grace, I was able to pay off my debt. I know God transformed my situation after years of financial bondage! I am debt-free and able to give generously and do more for His glory. I give God all the praise and glory for His direction and wisdom, and for you and your financial management course. May your ministry continue to be blessed as you speak God's word into our lives.

S.E., Canada

I would like to thank Tom Copland and Randy Ziegenhagel for their amazing teaching on Financial Management God's Way for Women through Copland Financial Ministries. I have learned how to manage my finances according to biblical principles. It has been an eye-opening experience for me. Thanks again! I am truly blessed!

R.G., Toronto, Ontario, Canada

It has given me great encouragement to take my financial situation more seriously and learn to manage money God's way. Thank you for holding these financial workshops. I didn't realize how much I needed to learn, grow, and change.

A.H., Canada

I'm participating in the Financial Management God's Way course and I am really enjoying it. I'm learning a lot and beginning to understand what I've been doing wrong all these years. Thanks so much for this awesome opportunity! May God richly bless you and your ministry.

Jean, Calgary, Alberta, Canada

I am blessed to be a part of this biblical teaching! God continues to make a difference in my life through this workshop series as applying biblical principles to my finances has affected other areas of my life, including improving my health and providing contentment and peace of mind. This teaching is exactly what I needed! As I have been learning and applying these financial truths, I have been sharing them with others. I have also purchased some of your books.

B.G., Saskatchewan, Canada

I dedicate this book to my Lord and Saviour, Jesus Christ, who called me to teach His word on finances.

My prayer is to continue to serve Him diligently and faithfully, "for God's gifts and his call are irrevocable" (Romans 11:29).

VI. DISCERNING GOD'S WILL THROUGH YOUR RELATIONSHIP WITH CHRIST   269

VII. CONCLUSION AND RECOMMENDED FOLLOW-UP   277

ABOUT THE AUTHOR

Tom Copland is a Chartered Professional Accountant (CPA) and servant of the Lord Jesus Christ, called to teach God's word on finances since 1982. Over the years, Tom has been privileged to help thousands learn and apply God's way of managing money. Through his teaching ministry and biblically based financial counseling, many individuals and couples have become debt-free and continue to do so!

Tom created the "Financial Moments" series, providing impactful one-minute summaries of biblical financial principles. To date, he has recorded 371 "Financial Moments" that currently air on 191 radio facilities and seven television stations across Canada and parts of the northern United States. It is estimated that over two million people hear at least one "Financial Moment" teaching per week.

In addition, Tom recorded almost 100 half-hour programs broadcast across 46 radio stations and seven television stations in Canada and parts of the northern United States.

Tom authored *Financial Management God's Way*, an in-depth study that teaches money management according to God's instructions in the Bible. Among the topics covered are how to get out of debt, a worldly versus a biblical view on money, budgeting, obtaining godly counsel, giving generously, investing, financial deceptions, stewardship, and how money management affects your relationship with God and your spouse.

In addition, Tom leads many workshops and webinars throughout the year. Topics include God's financial wisdom for business, biblically based estate planning, financial wisdom for young people, managing money during difficult times, discerning God's will for money management, and how the management of money impacts eternity.

Tom has produced helpful resources, such as the Copland Budgeting System. These resources are available on his website, www.coplandfinancialministries.org. Most of these resources can be accessed for free.

As a Chartered Professional Accountant, Tom owns and operates a public accounting firm in Markham, Ontario, Canada. Besides accounting and tax services, his firm offers biblically based financial advice. You may visit the firm's website at www.copland-ca.com.

ACKNOWLEDGMENTS

I would like to thank Henry Enriquez, my tech support, who has been faithful for over 25 years in giving of his time and expertise to help me with my ministry—performing a wide range of tasks too numerous to mention.

I extend a big thank you to Art Brooker, the chairman of the board of In Touch Ministries of Canada, who came up with the concept of the "Financial Moments." As well, I credit Art for putting me in contact with the appropriate individuals in radio and television to make the expansion of this ministry possible.

Additionally, I would like to thank Pastor Don Symons and Pastor Jack Hannah, the two pastors of my church, for being pillars of support, both personally and for the ministry to which God has called me. Further, I would like to thank my dear friend, Cam Golberg, who has been a great help over the years and a superb small group leader of the "Financial Management God's Way" series.

I am grateful to the financial coaches and small group leaders who volunteered to lead my in-depth study, "Financial Management God's Way," and taught hundreds of people how to handle money according to biblical principles. These leaders include Anthony Martino, Dan Tomlinson, Eli Papakirykos, Christine Kewallal, Liisa Snell, Randy Ziegenhagel, and Efrain Soto, who also translated a significant portion of my in-depth biblical financial study into Spanish.

Lastly, I am thankful to Julie Child for her excellent editing, and to Castle Quay Books for recognizing my vision and publishing this book.

PLEASE READ THIS BEFORE YOU BEGIN

My heart is to share how God has called me to teach His word on finances. Since 1982, the Lord has clearly revealed to me on many occasions what He created me to do. Psalm 139:13–16 states:

> For you created my inmost being;
>> you knit me together in my mother's womb.
> I praise you because I am fearfully and wonderfully made;
>> your works are wonderful,
>> I know that full well.
> My frame was not hidden from you
>> when I was made in the secret place,
>> when I was woven together in the depths of the earth.
> Your eyes saw my unformed body;
>> all the days ordained for me were written in your book
>> before one of them came to be.

In other words, when God created me in my mother's womb, He had a very specific plan and purpose for my life—to teach His word on finances. It's no coincidence then that I became a chartered accountant even before I came to know the Lord! After I accepted Jesus Christ as my Lord and Saviour on April 12, 1981, God revealed that His calling for my life was to teach and advise others how to manage the money entrusted to them according to biblical principles.

During my time on earth, I desire to serve the Lord faithfully and with all my effort, and I want to finish well before I go to be with the Lord for eternity. That's why I ask people to introduce me as a "servant of the Lord Jesus Christ." I don't believe I have any special talents; I'm simply a servant of the Lord, created and called to teach His word on finances (Ephesians 2:10; Romans 11:29).

The purpose of this book is to teach what the Bible says about finances. With over 2,300 references to money and material things, God's word contains incredible wisdom. Unfortunately, most people lack this wisdom and unintentionally violate biblical financial principles and later suffer the consequences.

However, once individuals and couples learn God's way of managing money and apply biblical financial principles to managing their monthly cash flow, they will be much better off financially in the long run. They will experience less financial stress and less marital conflict because of financial problems.

The most significant financial problem that people in North America and around the world have today is the accumulation of debt. It's been that way for decades and will likely be that way for decades more. Therefore, the primary purpose of this book is to teach biblical financial principles to equip people with the knowledge and wisdom they need to reduce debt, eventually become debt-free, and maintain a debt-free lifestyle.

When individuals learn the biblical financial principles and meditate on key Scriptures, God, through His word and His Spirit, will change the way they think about and manage money.

I've had the privilege of helping thousands of people learn what the Bible says on finances for over four decades, and I know from experience that if people learn and apply the biblical financial principles, they will get out of debt, develop a positive monthly cash flow, and experience God's peace in the area of finances (John 14:27).

INFLATION AND HIGHER INTEREST RATES

There is a major problem with rising inflation and higher interest rates in Canada, the United States, and worldwide at the time of writing this book. It is July 2022, and over the past nine months, the five-year fixed mortgage rate has risen from about 2 per cent to about 5.5 per cent. Consequently, mortgage rates have substantially increased for people with variable-rate mortgages, while fixed-rate mortgage holders will see their payments increase when their mortgage comes due for renewal. Sadly, many homeowners will no longer be able to afford their homes, forcing some to downsize, while others will lose their homes entirely, leaving them no choice but to rent.

At the same time, the inflation rate has reached its highest in over 39 years. Gas prices at the pump have doubled in the last two years, food prices have increased more than 10 per cent, and prices are rising on virtually everything. However, most individual salaries are *not increasing at the same rate as inflation*. When combined with the fact that most people will have significantly higher mortgage payments, many will experience severe financial trouble over the next few years for which they are not prepared.

However, for those who have learned and applied biblical financial principles, the changing economic tides and higher interest rates won't be near as concerning since they will carry minimal to no debt, which is God's directive (Proverbs 22:7; Deuteronomy 28). Further, if people follow God's wisdom in building some savings (Proverbs 21:20), they will have a cash surplus. Therefore, they are unlikely to suffer financially due to higher interest rates and inflation. They will also receive more interest income on their investments, such as guaranteed investment certificates. Clearly, it pays to manage money God's way!

Let me encourage you, it's never too late to learn God's word on finances, and that's what this book is all about! Finally, I recommend reading this book at least twice—the first time to learn the biblical financial principles and the second time to ensure you apply them in managing the money God has entrusted you.

I pray the Lord gives you His wisdom and guidance in implementing and applying these timeless biblical principles. They'll be of great value to you!

Tom Copland

INTRODUCTION

The biblical financial principles presented in this book and real-life case studies enable you to get your finances in order if diligently followed. Primary benefits include reducing and eventually eliminating debt and saving for future needs.

Of interest, the Bible contains about 500 verses on prayer, about 500 verses on faith, and an astounding 2,350 Scriptures that apply to money and material things. However, only about 3 per cent of those verses relate to giving, while around 97 per cent apply to other financial topics rarely taught in most churches.

Easy access to credit, including credit cards, personal lines of credit, bank overdrafts, zero per cent financing, retailer incentives, and relatively low interest rates, all entice us to borrow money. As a result, most people in our country and worldwide have spent more than they've earned and accumulated significant debt.

When you amass debt rather than savings, inevitably, at some point, *you will suffer the consequences.* Proverbs 22:3 states, "A prudent man foresees the difficulties ahead and prepares for them; the simpleton goes blindly on and suffers the consequences" (TLB).

Typically, when debt accumulates, most people try debt restructuring, such as obtaining a personal line of credit (perhaps collateralized against their home) and then paying off credit cards. But unfortunately, debt restructuring treats the symptoms and not the underlying problem. For example, people continue to regularly spend more than they earn and rack up even more debt.

I've seen thousands of cases where people attempt to refinance their debt through restructuring several times over a number of years. But sadly, the result is a mountain of debt and a worsened financial situation instead of savings for future needs. Once again, God's word provides timeless wisdom in Proverbs 21:20, stating, "The wise man saves for the future, but the foolish man spends whatever he gets" (TLB).

Since 1982, financial coaches with Copland Financial Ministries and myself have provided sound biblical financial advice to tens of thousands of people. As a result, I can confidently say that thousands have reduced their debt, with many becoming completely debt-free—no car loan, no line of credit, no credit card debt, and no mortgage!

Not surprisingly, no one has ever said, "Hey, Tom, we miss having all those loan payments." Instead, people usually offer thoughts like these:

"I never realized how much stress I was under because of our debt."

"An immense weight has come off my back now that I'm debt-free."

"It's great to be debt-free and have a surplus of money each month."

"Praise God! As my debt decreased, my stress level decreased, and I slept much better at night."

"Finally, I'm able to save for future needs, take that special family vacation, and give generously to God's work!"'

I have used numerous real-life case studies from the past four decades in this book to help you understand the practical application of biblical financial principles. It's essential that you learn and understand the biblical financial principles presented in God's word. Also, it's critical to implement those principles in managing the money and material things God has entrusted to you. First Corinthians 4:2 reminds us, "Now it is required that those who have been given a trust must prove faithful." James 1:22 states, "Do not merely listen to the word, and so deceive yourselves. Do what it says."

Because God's word contains extensive wisdom concerning money management, I quote many verses from the Bible. Christians usually feel comfortable with this. However, even if you're not a Christian, I encourage you to read through this book. I know from experience that you will benefit significantly in the long run if you learn and apply these biblical financial principles.

Positive outcomes of applying biblical financial principles include reducing or eliminating all debt and saving for future needs. In addition, it's important to establish an emergency fund to cover unforeseen expenses and events, like the loss of a job.

While reading this book, I encourage you to pray and ask God to speak to your heart and mind by His Holy Spirit, as God can highlight Scriptures to you. Psalm 119:105 specifies, "Your word is a lamp to my feet and a light for my path" (NCV).

God can also give you peace (John 14:27) or lack of peace concerning any proposed financial decision. May God direct you as you read through this book. May I remind you of the words in Isaiah 48:17, where God says, "I am the LORD your God, who teaches you what is good for you, who directs you in the way you should go."

I.

GOD'S WISDOM ON DEBT
AND THE IMPORTANCE OF SAVING

Most people carry a heavy debt load today. I've provided biblical counsel to thousands of individuals and couples since 1982, and so often, they asked, "How did we ever get into this mess?" Unfortunately, many have unintentionally spent more than they've earned and accumulated debt over several years.

Today, easy credit creates a phenomenal temptation to borrow and buy.

Like the warnings on cigarette packages about how smoking can be dangerous to your health, I would like to see this marked on every credit card!

There is nothing wrong with having a credit card. It is the *misuse* of credit cards that is the problem. Credit cards can easily allow individuals or couples to spend more than they earn and accumulate debt. The abuse of a credit card, a line of credit, or any form of debt can cause serious problems, for example:

1. Accumulated debt will often result in a poor credit rating so that when you apply for a mortgage, you could get turned down. If you're a renter, you may not be able to renew your lease or rent another place because many landlords run credit checks.
2. As your debt increases, your stress level increases. Therefore, debt can destroy your emotional and physical health because stress is often an underlying cause of sickness and disease, resulting in sleepless nights and health-related problems. However, if you follow

biblical financial principles, your stress level declines as your debt declines.

3. Marital relationships may become strained because debt accumulation is the primary reason couples argue. Sadly, the continued accumulation of debt often leads to separation and divorce.

4. Debt can adversely affect your spiritual health. As you accumulate debt, creditors could hound you with nasty letters and phone calls, causing considerable stress as you wonder how you're going to pay your loans. Inevitably, the financial strain distracts you from your relationship with God and ministry. In Matthew 6:24, Jesus said, "No one can serve two masters. Either you will hate the one and love the other, or you will be devoted to the one and despise the other. You cannot serve both God and money."

In summary, it's acceptable to have a credit card, but you need to use it cautiously and exercise self-control. Generally, only buy things you need, not things you merely want or desire. Also, make sure you can pay off your credit card balance each month. If you cannot pay it off each month, do whatever is necessary to stop using your credit card until it is paid off! Perhaps leave it at home, or use a debit card, which prevents you from spending money you don't have. A third option is to pay cash for all your minor expenses.

A. KEY BIBLICAL FINANCIAL PRINCIPLES IN DEALING WITH DEBT

Here are the fundamental biblical financial principles that deal with debt.

1. You Must Pay Your Debt

If you borrow money, God says you must pay it back. Psalm 37:21 says, "The wicked borrow and do not repay, but the righteous give generously." The NIRV puts it this way: "Sinful people borrow and don't pay back. But those who are godly give freely to others."

Note the distinction between a wicked or sinful person and a righteous or godly person. A sinful person borrows and does not repay, but the righteous person goes the second mile. The implication is that they pay their debts, and the righteous individual gives generously even when not required.

Further, Romans 13:8 states, "Let no debt remain outstanding, except the continuing debt to love one another, for whoever loves others has fulfilled the law." Payment of one's debts shows you care about the creditor.

2. When You Borrow, You Become a Servant to the Lender

When you borrow, especially a substantial amount of money, you will become a servant to the lender. Proverbs 22:7 states, "The rich rule over the poor, and the borrower is slave to the lender."

In other words, when you borrow money, you are committing yourself to "service the debt" for the term of the loan. Suppose you cannot pay off your loan; in that case, negative consequences could include a poor credit rating, repossession of your automobile, foreclosure on your home, and ineffectiveness as a Christian witness.

Further, when you borrow money, you can limit your future options.

Here are some examples:

1. A wife cannot stay home with the children and must continue to work full-time to service debt.
2. An individual cannot leave their secular job to work in ministry, as the ministry position pays less, and they need a higher income to service their debt.
3. Debt can easily cause stress, sleepless nights, and various health problems.
4. An older individual or couple cannot retire as planned but must continue to work to pay off their debt.

Never forget, you are the light of the world! In Matthew 5:14–16, Jesus said:

> You are the light of the world. A town built on a hill cannot be hidden. Neither do people light a lamp and put it under a bowl. Instead, they put it on its stand, and it gives light to everyone in the house. In the same way, let your light shine before others, that they may see your good deeds and glorify your Father in heaven.

Please consider what kind of Christian witness you will be in a dark world if you don't pay your debts or fail to pay on time. Likely, the person to whom you are witnessing won't take you seriously because you lost credibility in their eyes, as you didn't pay what you owed them.

As followers of Christ, we need to pay our debts and pay them on time, which is a genuine testimony for the Lord. Since becoming a Christian, I've intentionally paid everyone promptly. By doing so, I have successfully witnessed to many suppliers and creditors who might otherwise never attend a church or hear about Christ. By paying any outstanding debt and showing respect to lenders, many have been open to hearing the gospel message as I shared or taught biblical financial principles.

3. Borrowing Presumes on the Future

James 4:13–15 says:

> Now listen, you who say, "Today or tomorrow we will go
> to this or that city, spend a year there, carry on business
> and make money." Why, you do not even know what will
> happen tomorrow. What is your life? You are a mist that
> appears for a little while and then vanishes. Instead, you
> ought to say, "If it is the Lord's will, we will live and do this
> or that."

When you borrow money, you presume you will have sufficient
cash flow in the future to pay all your debt. Due to the uncertainty
of the future, there is always the risk of not being able to pay your
debt. As a result, you could experience significant consequences
and financial hardship.

Proverbs 27:1 states, "Do not boast about tomorrow, for you
do not know what a day may bring." Because only God knows
what's coming, every Christian must spend quality time with the
Lord in prayer, listening to God's voice to determine if it's His will
that you borrow money.

Jesus said, "My sheep listen to my voice; I know them, and
they follow me" (John 10:27). God has promised that he will
direct us (Psalm 32:8), and sometimes he speaks via a gentle
whisper (1 Kings 19:12).

4. God Promises to Meet Our Needs

In Matthew 6:31–33, Jesus tells us:

> "Do not worry, saying, 'What shall we eat?' or 'What shall
> we drink?' or 'What shall we wear?' For the pagans run
> after all these things, and your heavenly Father knows
> that you need them. But seek first his kingdom and his

righteousness, and all these things will be given to you as well."

Be encouraged that God promises to meet our needs—that is His responsibility. Our responsibility is to put Him first and to manage the money He has entrusted to us according to biblical financial principles and His specific will. Please note that God has promised to meet our needs, but *not necessarily our wants and desires*. At times, He may grant us our wants and desires, but that's not guaranteed.

Does God need a bank to accomplish this? The answer is no! In Philippians 4:19, Paul said, "My God will meet all your needs according to the riches of his glory in Christ Jesus." God, our heavenly Father, has promised to meet our needs as we put Him first. It is not the banks or credit card companies that meet our needs!

Of interest, I have searched the entire Bible many times, and I cannot find one place where God directed anyone to borrow money in order to provide for them or bless them. When the Creator of the universe provides, He is fully capable of doing so using His own resources since He is all-powerful, all-knowing, and omnipresent.

In summary, the God of the universe—King of kings and Lord of lords, who made the heavens and the earth—does not depend on a financial institution to meet your needs! He can provide supernaturally in any way and at any time He wants. Nevertheless, God could direct you to take on a mortgage to purchase a house, as long as you do so according to biblical principles, like developing a budget to ensure you can afford the payments. For more about this, be sure to check out the chapter in this book titled Questions to Consider Before Borrowing.

Furthermore, it's essential that any significant decisions you make are consistent with God's will. Note Luke 22:42, where

Jesus Himself called out to God, saying, "Father, if you are willing, take this cup from me; yet not my will, but yours be done."

5. God Promised the Israelites They Would Be Lenders and Not Borrowers if They Obeyed Him

In Deuteronomy 28:1–4, 8,12–13, we read:

> *If you fully obey the* LORD *your God* and carefully follow all his commands I give you today, the LORD your God will set you high above all the nations on earth. All these blessings will come on you and accompany you *if you obey the* LORD *your God*:
>
> You will be blessed in the city and blessed in the country.
>
> The fruit of your womb will be blessed, and the crops of your land and the young of your livestock—the calves of your herds and the lambs of your flocks…,
>
> The LORD will send a blessing on your barns and on everything you put your hand to. The LORD your God will bless you in the land he is giving you …
>
> The LORD will open the heavens, the storehouse of his bounty, to send rain on your land in season and to bless all the work of your hands. You will lend to many nations but will borrow from none. The LORD will make you the head, not the tail. If you pay attention to the commands of the LORD your God that I give you this day and carefully follow them, you will always be at the top, never at the bottom. (Emphasis added.)

What an incredible promise from the Lord! If we put Him first, He will bless us! And in the long-term, those who follow His biblical financial principles should be able to pay off all their debt and end up a lender and not a borrower.

If God's people do not follow His ways, they will not be blessed. Deuteronomy 28:15–18, 43–44, continues and says:

> However, *if you do not obey the* LORD *your God* and do not carefully follow all his commands and decrees I am giving you today, all these curses will come on you and overtake you:
>
> You will be cursed in the city and cursed in the country.
>
> Your basket and your kneading trough will be cursed.
>
> The fruit of your womb will be cursed, and the crops of your land, and the calves of your herds and the lambs of your flocks …
>
> The foreigners who reside among you will rise above you higher and higher, but you will sink lower and lower. They will lend to you, but you will not lend to them. They will be the head, but you will be the tail. (Emphasis added.)

In other words, if we do not fully obey the Lord our God in the realm of finances, meaning we are *not* managing money according to God's financial principles and God's specific will (Luke 22:42), then, as noted in Deuteronomy 28, we will not receive God's blessings, including financial benefits. It's interesting to note that these Scriptures used the word "cursed" five times and most of them relate to crops, calves, and lambs—implying financial difficulties for the farmers at that time.

In summary, God tells us He will bless us financially if we manage money His way. Indeed, God will meet our needs, and He may even bless us with a surplus. However, remember that God may also bless us in non-financial ways—with good health, a harmonious relationship with our spouse and children, or an influential career or ministry.

If we do not manage money God's way, all kinds of curses and problems could come upon us, and one of those problems could be the accumulation of debt.

In light of these biblical truths, it makes sense to learn what God's word says about finances, and then apply those truths to managing the money He has entrusted to you. It's equally important to pray regularly to discern how God wants you to handle *His* money.

6. All References in the Bible to Borrowing Are Negative

Please understand that it is not a sin to borrow; it is a sin to borrow and not repay. Once again, note Psalm 37:21: "The wicked borrow and do not repay, but the righteous give generously." In Romans 13:8, we learn that God clearly discourages the use of debt when Paul says "Let no debt remain outstanding."

All references in the Bible to borrowing are negative. Generally, debt was a curse at that time, and even today, it is a *form of a curse.* It's certainly not a blessing to be in debt. This perspective differs from the world's view that carrying debt is normal. For example, the worldly mindset considers it entirely acceptable to "buy now and pay later" and agrees that "smart people use other people's money."

These are financial deceptions, and the biblical truth is that smart people do not use other people's money. Instead, smart people use as little debt as possible and pay it off as quickly as they can!

In Scripture, God met needs without the aid of a lender. Here are some examples.

1. God provided food (manna) and water to the Israelites during their forty years in the desert (Exodus 16:35).

2. Jesus fed the five thousand with five loaves of bread and two fish (Mark 6:39–44), and there were even twelve baskets of food left over!
3. God used ravens to feed Elijah (1 Kings 17:4–6).
4. Working through Elijah, God provided flour and oil to the widow and her son during a famine (1 Kings 17:13–16).

King David said, "I was young and now I am old, yet I have never seen the righteous forsaken or their children begging bread" (Psalm 37:25). Before you borrow any money, I encourage you to spend quality time with the Lord in prayer, asking God to meet *your needs* and then wait for God's provision. Psalm 37:7 reminds us, "Be still before the LORD and wait patiently for him." The biblical truth is that God can fulfill your needs without you having to take on any debt!

Again, it is not a sin to borrow; it is a sin to borrow and not repay. However, God's best for you is to have no debt at all. I advise you to work towards that goal, no matter how long it takes.

7. Financial Turnarounds

The following are a few testimonies of significant financial turnarounds I've seen over the past four decades.

The first is a young couple who attended a series I led, "Debt Reduction God's Way." Their financial situation was quite common—having major credit card debt, a large personal line of credit, a mortgage, and two auto loans.

The key is they applied themselves to learning God's financial principles, including choosing to be content with less. They implemented a budget and used the surplus to pay down their debt. Within seven years, they were entirely debt-free, including no mortgage!

When the husband reached middle age, he felt led by the Lord to go into full-time ministry, and he could do that on a lower salary because he was debt-free. Today, he teaches others to manage money according to God's way. He emphasizes that when people borrow money, especially a lot of money, they put themselves under significant stress and limit their future options.

Another example is a single man who came to know the Lord in his late twenties. He had a lot of debt because he had unknowingly violated several biblical principles, which led to many sleepless nights. After listening to my teachings, he applied God's financial principles and discerned and followed God's specific will in managing the money entrusted to him. Within four years, he was completely debt-free, including having no mortgage! Praise God! Through His word and His Spirit, this man learned to think differently about money and therefore, to manage money according to biblical principles. God honored his obedience and blessed him incredibly.

The key Scriptures he relied on were Hebrews 4:12, which states, "The word of God is living and active. Sharper than any double-edged sword, it penetrates even to dividing soul and spirit, joints and marrow; it judges the thoughts and attitudes of the heart." And in John 10:27, Jesus said, "My sheep listen to my voice; I know them, and they follow me."

Another example is a single mother whose ex-husband left her with a limited income and significant debt. She diligently applied herself to learning biblical principles in managing her money, and God blessed her tremendously. For example, she ended up with unexpected income and a miraculous provision for her two children. Within twelve years, she was entirely debt-free! God is good!

These testimonies remind me of Psalm 107:8–9, which says, "Let them give thanks to the LORD for his unfailing love and his wonderful deeds for mankind, for he satisfies the thirsty and fills the hungry with good things."

8. Mr. Wise versus Mr. Unwise in Managing Money

Following is a list of the typical ways individuals manage money. For example, "Mr. Unwise" manages money the world's way, violating many biblical principles. On the other hand, "Mr. Wise" manages money God's way and experiences significant benefits in due course.

Mr. Unwise

1. Never saves; instead, borrows and buys.
2. Makes financial decisions based on personal desires or gut feelings, not needs.
3. Completes post-secondary education with significant debt.
4. Finances the purchase of a new car every several years.
5. Buys a home with very little down payment and takes on a large mortgage.
6. Furnishes his home using credit.
7. Fails to develop and implement a budget.
8. Usually runs a balance on his credit cards.

Mr. Wise

1. Develops a habit of saving for future needs.
2. Buys only what he needs and rarely what he wants and desires.
3. Saves for his education and completes university with little or no debt.
4. Drives a used car with no debt. If he were to buy a new car, he would keep it for its full lifetime and save for his next car in the interim.

5. Saves a significant down payment for a home and pays down the mortgage as quickly as possible.
6. Buys furniture (sometimes second-hand) for cash.
7. Lives within a set budget.
8. Uses a credit card carefully, pays off his balance each month, and incurs no interest charges.

9. The Importance of Saving

The key biblical principle provided in Proverbs 21:20 states, "The wise man saves for the future, but the foolish man spends whatever he gets" (TLB). As for the NIV, it says, "The wise store up choice food and olive oil, but fools gulp theirs down." Ultimately, God admonishes us to plan and save for future needs. It's very foolish, even dangerous, to spend everything you have.

Everyone should have some savings. How much savings should you have? As a practical matter, I would suggest that most individuals and couples have sufficient savings to provide for six to nine months of necessary expenditures. You never know when you or your spouse might be out of work or incur a sudden unexpected expense.

Unfortunately, most people do not have any savings, so when an unexpected expenditure (or even one that is expected, like an annual insurance premium or vacation) comes along, they are forced into debt because they have not saved the funds.

For instance, few people save up to replace their automobile, even though everyone knows it will eventually wear out. If you don't plan and save for your next auto replacement, you will have a car loan for your entire life.

Form #3 of the Copland Budgeting System can project these non-monthly expenses and incorporate them into your monthly budget, on form #5. I encourage you to download the Copland

Budgeting System if you haven't already. It's Excel-based and available on our website at www.coplandfinancialmistries.org at no cost. In addition, a 30-minute video explains how to use it.

10. God's Admonition That We Should Plan Ahead

What did Jesus warn us to do in the parable of the tower? How does this apply to saving for future needs? In Luke 14:28–30, Jesus said:

> "Suppose one of you wants to build a tower. Won't you first sit down and estimate the cost to see if you have enough money to complete it? For if you lay the foundation and are not able to finish it, everyone who sees it will ridicule you, saying, 'This person began to build and wasn't able to finish.'"

Of course, most of us are *not* planning to build a tower. However, you may be planning to save for a down payment on a house, for your children's future education, or perhaps for your retirement.

The main biblical principle is this—Christ admonishes us to plan ahead!

From a financial perspective, the most practical way to plan your finances is to develop and implement a budget. The purpose of budgeting is to ensure you spend less than you earn and have a surplus to pay down debt and save for future needs.

Unfortunately, only about 5 to 10 per cent of people have a workable budget. Most people manage their finances based on personal desires and guesswork, which is dangerous. Here's something I strongly encourage you to consider. Review these key Scriptures for yourself, and you will find that my summary is accurate.

We know that God's perspective of saving for future needs opposes the world's perspective to buy now and pay later. God is in control, and his word in Psalm 103:19, says, "The LORD has established His throne in the heavens, and His sovereignty rules over all" (NASB). You don't have to worry since God (not the bank or credit card company) has promised to meet your needs as you put Him first. God is your ultimate source of provision for all things. Note Matthew 6:31–33, where Jesus said:

> "Do not worry, saying, 'What shall we eat?' or 'What shall we drink' or 'What shall we wear?' For the pagans run after all these things, and your heavenly Father knows that you need them. But seek first his kingdom and his righteousness, and all these things will be given to you as well."

Considering God's promises regarding finances, is it not reasonable for followers of Christ to trust God to meet their needs rather than relying on credit cards, personal lines of credit, and other loans?

Of course, it is! Proverbs 3:5–6, reminds us to "trust in the LORD with all your heart and lean not on your own understanding; in all your ways submit to him, and he will make your paths straight."

11. A Summary: Biblical Perspective versus Worldly Perspective

The biblical perspective is to save regularly for the future and trust God's provision and perfect timing. The world believes that it is acceptable to "buy now and pay later" and that "smart people use other people's money," which is contrary to God's word. God's perspective is that smart people use as little debt as possible and pay it off as quickly as possible!

B. MEMORY VERSES

The following are my suggested Scriptures on which to meditate.

Keep this Book of the Law always on your lips; meditate on it day and night, so that you may be careful to do everything written in it. Then you will be prosperous and successful. (Joshua 1:8)

The rich rule over the poor, and the borrower is slave to the lender. (Proverbs 22:7)

My God will meet all your needs according to the riches of his glory in Christ Jesus. (Philippians 4:19)

As you meditate on Scripture, God, through His word (Hebrews 4:12) and His Spirit (John 10:27), transforms how you think about money and material things. In this way, you will manage money in God's way, not according to worldly standards.

C. CASE STUDIES, QUESTIONS, TOM'S COMMENTS

To help you understand how biblical principles can be applied practically, I will provide several case studies. People often relate some of these everyday situations to their personal finances. For example, after speaking at a church or leading a workshop, I have had people tell me, "Tom, I thought you were talking about me when you gave that example!"

Of course, I was not explicitly talking about them, nor did I know anything about their personal finances. I was merely giving examples of typical scenarios I've seen hundreds of times. For the following case studies, I randomly selected the people's names.

12. Case Study #1: Mike and Sharon Accumulate Debt

Mike and Sharon are Christians. Over several years, they accumulated significant credit card debt. With interest rates as high as 28 per cent, they felt they could solve their problem by restructuring their debt. They obtained a personal line of credit from their bank at a much lower interest rate and used the funds to pay off their credit cards.

Further, to play it safe, and at their bank's suggestion, they set the limit on their line of credit at an amount greater than their total credit card liabilities to have a buffer should they need more funds in the future.

For a while, they believed they had solved their financial problems. However, over the next few years, the balance on their line of credit gradually reached its limit. Again, they met with their banker.

Since their home had gone up in value, the bank agreed to give them a second mortgage on their home to pay down their line of credit. The second mortgage reduced their monthly payments, but it extended the payment term for their first mortgage, resulting in additional interest charges. Unfortunately, their financial adviser had not explained this to them.

Over the next few years, the balance owing on their credit cards and line of credit again increased. However, because their home had decreased in value during this time, the bank would not lend them any more money.

Consequently, they were forced to withdraw money from their retirement fund, resulting in two new problems: first, a tax liability because of the retirement fund withdrawal, and second, a significant concern that they would not have sufficient money for retirement.

Here are some questions to consider. Before reading my comments, think about your answers and write your suggested solutions in the space provided. Please give a relevant Scripture reference where possible.

QUESTION #1

Did Mike and Sharon's debt restructuring vis-à-vis the personal line of credit and second mortgage solve their financial problems?

TOM'S COMMENT

No! The debt restructuring did not solve their financial problems because *their overspending continued after debt restructuring*, and they ended up with even more debt.

QUESTION #2

Can you identify the underlying problems this couple is struggling with? Could there be a spiritual issue? Provide a reference to Scripture for each point.

TOM'S COMMENT

The real underlying issue for Mike and Sharon is that they violated many biblical financial principles. Their problem is likely spiritual in nature. Some of the biblical principles they broke are:

1. They showed a lack of contentment as they spent more than they earned over many years (see 1 Timothy 6:6–8).
2. They did not develop and implement a budget (see Luke 14:28–30).
3. They took on too much debt (see Proverbs 22:7).
4. They were unwilling to sacrifice as needed (see Luke 9:23).

5. They did not know their financial status (see Proverbs 27:23).
6. They were not diligent in planning their finances, especially concerning debt accumulation (see Proverbs 21:5).
7. They did not foresee future financial problems, even after restructuring their debt a second time (see Proverbs 22:3).

QUESTION #3

Was it wrong for Mike and Sharon to get a personal line of credit at first? What benefit did the line of credit provide?

TOM'S COMMENT

No, it was not wrong to do that, given their situation. The personal line of credit lowered their interest costs and reduced their monthly payments.

QUESTION #4

What course of action do you believe Mike and Sharon should take to get their finances in order? Note there are several things they should do. Please provide a reference to Scripture.

TOM'S COMMENT

Most importantly, Mike and Sharon need to learn and implement God's financial principles, as stated in James 1:22, "Do not merely listen to the word, and so deceive yourselves. Do what it says."

For example, I would advise them to take part in my in-depth biblical financial study, "Financial Management God's Way."

This study is available in a small group by Zoom. If you are interested in taking this course, and would like information on how to register, visit www.coplandfinancialministries.org.

In addition, this couple should:

- Develop and implement a budget to spend less than their income and use the surplus to pay down debt (see Luke 14:28–30).
- Record their expenses (suggested form #6 of the Copland Budgeting System), so they understand where their money is going and their financial facts (see Proverbs 27:23).
- Meditate on Scriptures related to their problem areas (see Joshua 1:8).
- Learn to be content and live within their income (see Philippians 4:11–13).
- Save money for unexpected expenses (see Proverbs 21:20).
- Seek godly financial advice, first from God Himself (see 1 Kings 22:5), second from God's word (see Psalm 119:24), and third from a wise and godly financial adviser (1 Corinthians 2:14–15). Note that the banker in this case provided unwise, non-biblical financial advice.
- Because credit cards create a temptation for Mike and Sharon to spend more than they earn, they should perform *plastic surgery* on their credit cards by cutting them up! (see 1 Corinthians 10:13). A better plan would be to use cash or debit to pay for future purchases.

QUESTION #5

What do you think the consequences would be if Mike or Sharon were out of work for some time?

TOM'S COMMENT

Disastrous! They have no savings and spend more than they earn, so their monthly cash flow deficit would increase substantially, and their debt would accumulate at an even faster rate. The resulting financial stress would negatively affect their marriage, and if it continued, it could result in separation or divorce. We at Copland Financial Ministries are committed to helping couples avoid this pitfall.

Consider the relevance and application of the following Bible verse concerning Mike and Sharon's situation. Write your comments below.

"The wise man saves for the future, but the foolish man spends whatever he gets" (Proverbs 21:20 TLB).

TOM'S COMMENT

Mike and Sharon fall into the *foolish* category as they have been spending all their income, and then some, and not saving for future needs. They need to develop and implement a budget to ensure they spend less than they earn and use the surplus to pay down debt and save for future needs.

13. Case Study #2: A Young Single Man

Sam is a young single man who lives with his parents and pays a relatively small amount for room and board. Although he has worked full-time for approximately three years, Sam earns an average salary and has very little savings.

Sam noticed that the price of homes in his area increased significantly over several years and wondered if it made sense to purchase a house or condominium of his own. He spoke to Peter, a friend and real estate agent from his church.

Peter enthusiastically explained to Sam why real estate was the most profitable investment—a "sure thing"—and that he would make a lot of money over the next few years. When Sam expressed concerns that he had no significant down payment, Peter said this was not a problem as he could help him arrange the financing. Finally, Peter instructed Sam to "step out in faith" and "trust God" for the mortgage payments. Sam took his advice, purchased a house, and assumed a substantial mortgage.

For a while, everything seemed fine as the market value of Sam's home increased, and he was able to make his mortgage payments. However, about three years later, Sam ran into financial difficulty.

Sam did not prepare a budget before buying his house, and he did not consider all the hidden costs of homeownership. So it surprised him when he tallied up all his costs three years later. The total cost of maintaining the home, including utilities, repairs, maintenance, property taxes, insurance, and mortgage payments, was much greater than he expected.

Unfortunately, Sam spent more than he earned and accumulated debt. His situation was further complicated when the real estate market declined during the same period, and his house decreased in value.

QUESTION #1
What biblical and practical mistakes did Sam make before purchasing the house? Hint: Read Luke 14:28–30 and Proverbs 24:3.

TOM'S COMMENT

Before Sam bought his house, he did not prepare a budget to assess its affordability (see Luke 14:28–30). Furthermore, Sam did not have all the facts. For example, he did not have knowledge of the costs associated with the house before committing to the purchase (see Proverbs 24:3–4).

QUESTION #2

Did Peter provide credible, biblical counsel? Please explain your answer and provide references to Scripture.

TOM'S COMMENT

No, Peter had a conflict of interest in that he would benefit by receiving a commission from Sam's decision to purchase a house (see Philippians 2:3–4). Peter's counsel was unbiblical because he advised Sam to assume more debt than Sam could afford. Peter was excited about selling a house but did not assess Sam's ability to pay (see Proverbs 19:2). On the other hand, Sam did not seek and obtain godly counsel from more than one source (see Proverbs 14:15; 5:22).

QUESTION #3

Did Sam seek the counsel of the Lord? Did he spend considerable time in prayer with God, seeking God's will for his life regarding this critical decision? Should he have? Please provide a reference to Scripture.

TOM'S COMMENT

Sam did not pray and seek the counsel of the Lord before purchasing when he should have. In 1 Kings 22:5, we read that "Jehoshaphat also said to the king of Israel, 'First seek the counsel of the LORD.'"

QUESTION #4

Did Sam study what God's word had to say on debt beforehand? Should he have? What would have likely occurred if he consulted God's word before purchasing a house? Please provide Scriptural references as applicable.

TOM'S COMMENT

Sam did not study God's word on debt, because if he had, he would have understood that God discourages debt (see Proverbs 22:7) and that borrowing presumes on the future (see James 4:13–15), God promises to meet our needs (see Philippians 4:19), and God requires that we plan in advance by preparing a budget to determine if we can afford something (see Luke 14:28–30). If Sam had followed God's biblical principles, he would have avoided the financial difficulties he experienced by taking on too much debt.

QUESTION #5

What do you think about Peter's advice to "step out in faith" and "trust God" for the loan payments?

TOM'S COMMENT

This advice was worldly and in Peter's self-interest (see James 3:16). Given that Sam did not pray and seek the counsel of the Lord and did not consult God's word regarding such an important decision, it is reasonable to conclude that Sam did not step out in faith, trusting God concerning the purchase. It's more likely that Sam trusted Peter's advice and his own personal judgment.

QUESTION #6

Note, this is the most important question for this case study.

What prerequisites should be met before a committed Christian genuinely steps out in faith and borrows a significant amount of money? Please provide references to Scripture.

TOM'S COMMENT

A Christian should step out in faith only after doing the following:

- In prayer, sincerely ask God for wisdom (James 1:5) and specific direction (Psalm 32:8) for your life.
- Be committed to doing God's will and not your own will (Luke 22:42).
- Study what God's word says concerning such decisions (Psalm 119:105) and concerning debt (Deuteronomy 28:1–44), God's promise to meet our needs (Matthew 6:31–33), and the warning to repay (Psalm 37:21).
- The most practical step is to prepare a budget to determine if you can afford it (Proverbs 21:5).
- Obtain counsel from godly financial advisers (1 Corinthians 2:14–15) and your spouse, if applicable (Genesis 2:24).

• Only proceed after you have spent sufficient time with the Lord in prayer, waiting upon God (Psalm 37:7), and only after receiving His peace regarding such a critical decision (John 14:26–27).

QUESTION #7

Consider the relevance and application of the following verses regarding Sam's situation. Write your comments below each verse.

"I will instruct you and teach you in the way you should go; I will counsel you with my loving eye on you" (Psalm 32:8).

TOM'S COMMENT

God has promised that He will personally direct His children. But unfortunately, Sam did not spend quality time with the Lord in prayer, seeking God's direction before buying the house.

"Plans fail for lack of counsel, but with many advisers they succeed" (Proverbs 15:22).

TOM'S COMMENT

Sam's plans failed because Sam did not follow God's wisdom in obtaining advice from several advisers. Instead, Sam took a straightforward approach by believing the biased advice of the real estate agent.

"The simple believe anything, but the prudent give thought to their steps" (Proverbs 14:15).

TOM'S COMMENT
Sam was not prudent by receiving biblical financial advice from someone independent of getting a commission and who had a good understanding of God's word on finances.

14. In Summary: God's Wisdom on Debt and Saving

The Scriptures and practical, real-life case studies show that God's word clearly discourages debt, warns of the dangers of debt (Proverbs 22:7), and admonishes you to plan, which means to prepare a budget to ensure you can afford something before you make a purchase (Luke 14:28–30).

In addition, the emphasis in God's word is not to borrow and buy but rather to save for future needs as much as practical (Proverbs 21:20). We all need savings for those rainy days in the event of unforeseen expenditures or a job loss. Therefore, it's prudent to start saving for future expenses you can anticipate, such as an automobile replacement, down payment for a house, children's education, or retirement.

To learn more about God's wisdom on debt and the importance of saving, check out www.coplandfinancialministries.org. There are an incredible number of resources there, and most are free. In addition, you can follow us on Facebook, Instagram, and Twitter at @Biblefinance.

Finally, it's essential to understand the biblical principles concerning debt and saving. However, if you are already in debt, like most people, it's critical to know how to get out of debt, and that is what the next chapter covers.

II

HOW TO GET OUT OF DEBT

From the previous chapter, we know that God discourages debt and warns of the dangers of debt. It is reasonable then to conclude that God's best is for all people to develop and implement a plan to become debt-free.

Since 1982, I've helped thousands of people learn and apply God's financial principles. For those who *diligently* learned and implemented the biblical principles in managing money, almost all reduced their debt significantly, and many became entirely debt-free! No one has ever regretted it.

A. SEVEN PRACTICAL STEPS TO HELP YOU GET OUT OF DEBT

1. Pray and Ask God for His Wisdom and Specific Direction

We often don't know what to do when making critical financial decisions. The good news is that God knows what we should do, and He is willing to give us his incredible wisdom! James 1:5–7 states:

> If any of you lacks wisdom, you should ask God, who gives generously to all without finding fault, and it will be given to you. But when you ask, you must believe and not doubt, because the one who doubts is like a wave of the sea, blown and tossed by the wind. That person should not expect to receive anything from the Lord.

God's wisdom is infinite; ours is not. Remember, He is all-knowing, all-powerful, and omnipresent—in other words, present everywhere. God knows the future, but we do not (Isaiah 46:10).

Furthermore, God knows our needs, and He promised to meet those needs *if* we put Him first (Matthew 6:31–33). Putting God first in our lives involves learning to manage money according to His principles and His specific will. A part of that process is developing and implementing a financial plan to become debt-free.

Regarding the specifics of that financial plan, God has promised to direct you all the way. In Psalm 32:8, God said, "I will instruct you and teach you in the way you should go; I will counsel you with my loving eye on you."

From the Scriptures, we can see that God will impart His wisdom and direction as to how you can get out of debt. This requires that you ask Him in faith, take time to pray, earnestly read His word, listen to His voice, and *discern* His specific will (Psalm 25:12).

Further, in John 10:27, Jesus said, "My sheep listen to my voice; I know them, and they follow me." God may not speak audibly to you, but He will speak to you through His word (Psalm 119:105), His Holy Spirit (John 16:13), and biblical counsel (Psalm 1:1–3; 1 Corinthians 2:14–15), *if* you genuinely desire to manage money God's way.

2. Study and Meditate on God's Word as It Relates to Finances and Implement God's Financial Principles in Your Life

The Bible contains about 500 verses on faith and 500 verses on prayer, which are clearly vital topics. However, an impressive

2,350 references apply to money and material things. Further, sixteen of Christ's parables apply to money management.

God knew that financial management would be a significant challenge for many and that the world's way of managing money would be contrary to His way. So, God provided us with sound financial biblical truths in His word (John 8:31–32).

The psalmist makes the following comments concerning God's word: "Your statutes are my delight; they are my counselors (Psalm 119:24), and, "Your word is a lamp for my feet, a light on my path" (Psalm 119:105).

Then, concerning meditating on God's word, He instructs us: "Keep this Book of the Law always on your lips; meditate on it day and night, so that you may be careful to do everything written in it. Then you will be prosperous and successful" (Joshua 1:8).

When an individual or couple gets into financial difficulty, it is almost always because they violated one or more of God's financial principles, usually unknowingly. Some examples include:

- Not having any savings for an emergency. Proverbs 21:20 (TLB) states, "The wise man saves for the future, but the foolish man spends whatever he gets."
- Taking on too much debt. Proverbs 22:7 warns that you may become a slave to the lender, and of course, we are here to serve God, not a lender!
- Co-signing a loan, which the Bible warns against. Proverbs 11:15 (CEV) states, "It's a dangerous thing to guarantee payment for someone's debts. Don't do it!"
- Getting involved in an investment they did not understand (Proverbs 19:2), and that was not biblically diversified (Ecclesiastes 11:1–2).
- Not following a budget (Luke 14:28–30) and making financial decisions based on guesswork and personal desires rather than financial facts.

Many times, the resulting financial stress could have been avoided by simply following the counsel and wisdom of God's word, the Bible. James 1:22 reminds us, "Do not merely listen to the word, and so deceive yourselves. Do what it says."

3. Evaluate Your Present Financial Position: Assets, Liabilities, Revenues, and Expenses

Scripture tells us, "Be sure you know the condition of your flocks, give careful attention to your herds" (Proverbs 27:23). Most people were farmers when this proverb was written, so the modern-day application of this biblical principle is that we need to know where we stand financially. In other words, you need to understand all aspects of your finances, including your assets, liabilities (with payment terms and interest rates), and revenues such as salary.

Further, it's essential to track your expenses to know where your money is going. This means that you must know your financial facts. Financial decisions based on guesswork, gut feelings, or personal desires are very dangerous and can easily result in major financial problems.

The majority of people spend all their regular income and have no idea where their money has gone. I've counseled thousands over four decades, and I've seen that when they start tracking their expenses, there are often some big surprises! Many are shocked to learn they spend more on unnecessary expenditures than realized. Undoubtedly, a habit of overspending contributes to a significant portion of their accumulated debt.

4. Develop and Implement a Budget

In the late 1980s, I did an in-depth study of what the Bible says about planning. I found approximately forty scriptural references to planning, and generally, they admonish us to plan ahead. For example, according to Jesus in the Parable of the Tower (Luke 14:28–30), failing to plan ahead is foolish.

The most practical tool to plan your finances effectively is a budget. A correctly implemented budget will enable you to spend less than your income each month, which will give you a surplus to pay down debt and save for future needs.

In addition, it is wise to apply a large portion of lump-sum receipts (like income tax refunds, monetary gifts, and bonuses) to either debt reduction or savings. I can't emphasize enough that there is no substitute for developing and implementing a budget to reduce debt and pave the road to debt-free living!

5. Learn to Be Content with God's Provision

Learning to be content to live within God's provision for you is a significant challenge for many, and it's often the most challenging step to becoming debt-free. The issue is that most people regularly spend more than they earn, meaning they live beyond their means.

When someone spends more than they earn over a long time, it's usually because of a lack of contentment—they are not content to live within the income or resources God has provided. This heart issue can also reveal itself in the form of selfishness, covetousness, or greed. All three are contrary to God's word (Philippians 2:3–4; Exodus 20:17; Luke 12:15). This topic will be covered more extensively in the later chapter, Developing Godly Attitudes Towards Money.

When individuals spend more than they regularly earn, they must learn contentment. Even the apostle Paul had to learn to be content! Here is what Paul said in Philippians 4:11–13:

I have learned to be content whatever the circumstances. I know what it is to be in need, and I know what it is to have plenty. I have learned the secret of being content in any and every situation, whether well fed or hungry, whether living in plenty or in want. I can do all this through him who gives me strength.

Consider this: What was Paul's *secret* to learning content- ment? Consider that before writing your answer below or looking at my comments.

TOM'S COMMENT

Paul learned to be content, first by depending on God. It was God who gave Paul the wisdom, direction, and strength he needed to learn to be content. In other words, it was Paul's personal rela- tionship with Jesus Christ that was key to learning contentment.

Further, Paul focused on things of eternal value rather than the temporal, as demonstrated in Colossians 3:1–2, where Paul said: "Since, then, you have been raised with Christ, set your hearts on things above, where Christ is, seated at the right hand of God. Set your minds on things above, not on earthly things."

God generally teaches us contentment through circumstances, by His Holy Spirit, and His word. In the long run, we will be less frustrated and much happier when we choose to be content with God's provision and specific will for our lives. First Timothy 6:6–8 states, "Godliness with contentment is great gain. For we brought nothing into the world, and we can take nothing out of it. But if we have food and clothing, we will be content with that."

6. With Your Surplus Cash, Pay Off the Most Expensive Debt and Non-Deductible Debt First

As you implement your budget and develop a cash surplus each month, pay down the debt with the highest interest rate first— usually your credit cards. When that debt is paid, tackle the next debt with the highest interest rate, and so on, until all your debt is gone.

In addition, it makes sense to pay down your "non-deductible debt" first; then pay down debt where the interest is tax-deductible. It is God's best that all debts be paid in full as soon as possible, whether the interest is deductible or not.

To explain, in Canada, interest expense can be deducted on funds borrowed and used for business or investment purposes. However, you cannot deduct interest on loans where the funds have been invested into your registered retirement savings plan. So those loans are considered "non-deductible debt." Because interest expense on "deductible debt" can be deducted in deter- mining your taxable income, then the after-tax cost of that inter- est expense is reduced by the amount of the income tax saved.

For example, let's assume that your personal marginal income tax rate is 30 per cent, and the interest rate on a particular busi- ness or investment loan is 5 per cent (this interest is deductible for tax purposes). Then your after-tax cost on that loan is 3.5 per cent. So, the difference of 1.5 per cent represents your tax savings calculated as your 30 per cent marginal tax rate times 5 per cent interest rate on the loan.

Therefore, assuming the interest rates are the same, it is best to pay off non-deductible debt before you pay off deductible debt because deductible debt has a lower after-tax cost.

Also, before paying down debt early, especially your mortgage, determine if there are any early payment penalties under the agreement. If so, calculate the implications of those penalties.

When the penalties are significant (like three months of payments for certain mortgages), it makes sense not to incur those significant penalties but rather to save money until your mortgage comes due. Then, at that point, apply those funds against your mortgage principal.

In the future, always negotiate flexible repayment terms on any debt so that any cash surplus can be used for debt reduction without penalties.

7. Depend on God, Follow Through, and Persevere Until You Are Debt-Free

Generally, it takes several years to become debt-free. While paying off your debt, it is critical to depend entirely on God to enable you to follow through. If you attempt to become debt-free in your own strength, relying on your own knowledge and wisdom, you will likely have limited success.

Not only that, you will miss out on the invaluable opportunity to develop a deeper intimacy with God as you work through this process. Since God is all-powerful, all-knowing, and omnipresent, He alone can give you the perseverance, insight, and direction needed to become debt-free. I have seen this happen thousands of times!

In John 15:5, Jesus said, "I am the vine; you are the branches. If you remain in me and I in you, you *will bear much fruit; apart from me you can do nothing*" (emphasis added). In Isaiah 46:4, God promised: "Even to your old age and gray hairs I am he, I am he who will sustain you. I have made you and I will carry you; I will sustain you and I will rescue you."

Even if finance is not your area of expertise, God promises to provide what you need. In 2 Corinthians 12:9, Jesus said, "My grace is sufficient for you, for my power is made perfect in weakness."

Since 1982, I have had the privilege of helping thousands of people learn and apply God's financial principles and discern God's specific will for their financial decisions. As a result, thousands have reduced their debt, and thousands have become totally debt-free! Matthew 19:26 reminds us, "With man this is impossible, but with God all things are possible."

I strongly encourage you and your spouse, if you are married, to commit to these seven practical steps to become completely debt-free! May the Lord guide you as you look to Him for wisdom, understanding, direction, and the perseverance you need to reach your goals.

8. Summary of the Steps to Get Out of Debt
- Pray and ask God for his wisdom and specific direction.
- Study and meditate on God's word related to finances, and implement God's financial principles in your life.
- Evaluate your present financial position—assets, liabilities, revenues, and expenses.
- Develop and implement a budget (Luke 14:28–30).
- Learn to be content with God's provision.
- With your surplus cash, pay off the most expensive debt and any non-deductible debt first.
- Depend on God, follow through, and persevere until you are debt-free.

9. The Importance of Meditating Upon Scripture
I encourage people to meditate on God's word because God, through His word and Spirit, can change the way people think about and manage money. Hebrews 4:12–13 states:

The word of God is alive and active. Sharper than any double-edged sword, it penetrates even to dividing soul and spirit, joints and marrow; it judges the thoughts and attitudes of the heart. Nothing in all creation is hidden from God's sight. Everything is uncovered and laid bare before the eyes of him to whom we must give account.

Further, 2 Timothy 3:16–17 states: "All Scripture is God-breathed and is useful for teaching, rebuking, correcting and training in righteousness, so that the servant of God may be thoroughly equipped for every good work."

B. SUGGESTED MEMORY VERSE

"If you fully obey the LORD your God and carefully follow all his commands I give you today … The LORD will open the heavens, the storehouse of his bounty, to send rain on your land in season and to bless all the work of your hands. You will lend to many nations but will borrow from none" (Deuteronomy 28:1,12).

C. CASE STUDIES, QUESTIONS, TOM'S COMMENTS

10. Case Study #1: A Couple Learns God's Way of Managing Money

Jim and Jennifer are a married couple who earn average incomes. By the end of their first year of marriage, they noticed their credit card balances had risen. However, they were not overly concerned and dismissed it as a few one-time expenses they incurred as newlyweds.

However, over the next two years, the balances on their credit cards and personal line of credit increased substantially. They were alarmed and did not understand why this was happening.

As a result, they attended a small-group, in-depth biblical financial study through their church. They were amazed at how much God's word had to say on finances! Jim and Jennifer realized they had *unknowingly* violated many biblical principles concerning money management.

Over the following months, they prioritized learning what God's word said about finances. Next, they recorded all their expenses for two months, which revealed a pattern of spending more than they earned. This explained why their debt had increased. Finally, Jim and Jennifer developed and implemented a budget to ensure they spent less than they earned going forward. Then they used the surplus to pay down their debt.

Jim and Jennifer focused on paying off their credit cards first, as the interest rates were high. They destroyed two credit cards and only kept one each. They agreed not to use their credit cards unless absolutely necessary.

Next, they attacked their personal line of credit while reducing their overall expenses. Although this was not easy, they prayed and trusted God to help them learn to be content with less to get their finances in order (see Philippians 4:11–13).

Within three years, Jim and Jennifer had paid off all their credit card and line of credit debt! Both felt like a heavy weight had lifted off their backs as they had not realized the sheer burden of their debt load.

However, they were not satisfied to stop there. They developed a new budget to apply any cash surplus against their mortgage as they learned that by paying just $400 per month extra against their mortgage, they would save about $50,000 in interest costs!

In addition, they would be completely debt-free in less than ten years!

Jim and Jennifer regularly thank God for the financial wisdom in His word and how He enabled them to learn and apply biblical financial principles, including learning to be content with a minimized lifestyle.

Another exciting point is that they glorified God through obedience to His word concerning finances and being a powerful Christian witness to others.

I recommend you answer all the following questions to the best of your ability before reviewing my comments. Provide a reference to Scripture to support your answer.

QUESTION #1

What actions did Jim and Jennifer initially take that were inconsistent with God's principles? Please provide a Scripture reference for each point.

TOM'S COMMENT

Concerning the actions Jim and Jennifer initially took that were *inconsistent* with Scripture:

- They did not know where they spent their money (see Proverbs 27:23).
- They were unaware their spending exceeded their income; therefore, they accumulated debt (see Proverbs 22:7).
- They did not develop and implement a budget (see Luke 14:28–30).
- They were not content to live within God's provision (see 1 Timothy 6:6–8).

- They had no savings or emergency fund for unexpected expenditures (see Proverbs 21:20).
- They were not aware of what God's word had to say on finances (see Psalm 119:105).
- They did not seek God's counsel (see 1 Kings 22:5).
- They did not obtain counsel from a godly financial adviser (see Proverbs 15:22; Psalm 1:1–3).
- They made financial decisions based on guesswork and personal desires rather than their financial facts (see Proverbs 24:3).

QUESTION #2

What actions did Jim and Jennifer display that were *consistent* with biblical financial management? Provide a Scripture reference for each point.

TOM'S COMMENT

- They studied and implemented God's word on finances (see Joshua 1:8).
- They understood their financial position, such as their debt load and where their money was being spent (see Proverbs 27:23).
- They diligently planned their finances using a budget (see Proverbs 21:5).
- They made debt reduction a priority (see Deuteronomy 28:1, 12).
- They reduced the temptation of easy credit by destroying two credit cards and used one card only when necessary (see 1 Corinthians 10:13).

- They sacrificed by minimizing their lifestyle (see Luke 9:24).
- They learned contentment by depending on God (see Philippians 4:11–13).
- They persevered with debt reduction (see James 1:4).
- They depended on God to implement His financial principles (see John 15:5).
- They regularly thanked God for His financial wisdom and for enabling them to be content with a reduced lifestyle (see Psalm 118:1).

QUESTION #3

What do you think Jim and Jennifer will experience in their finances when their mortgage is paid off?

TOM'S COMMENT

They will likely feel an enormous sense of relief and accomplishment! In addition, they will experience freedom and the flexibility to do other things, like giving more generously to God's work and saving for retirement. Most certainly, they will sense God's blessing in their lives.

QUESTION #4

Review "Schedule A" (at the end of this chapter) of Jim and Jennifer's financial situation before implementing God's word on finances. List the expenses you think they could decrease and by how much.

TOM'S COMMENT

As demonstrated in "Schedule A" for Jim and Jennifer's expenses, they did the following to create a monthly positive cash flow.

- Sold one of their two automobiles and shared the other.
- Reduced their entertainment and recreational costs substantially.
- Bought discounted groceries.
- Used caution when making purchases, asking themselves if the item was a need or a desire.
- Jim did more of the auto repairs and house maintenance himself.
- Chose not to travel for three years, and took inexpensive day trips during holidays instead.
- Canceled their gym memberships and exercised at home.
- Jennifer reduced clothing expenses, and Jim stopped buying new tools.

As you can see, Jim and Jennifer originally had a $700 per month cash-flow deficit. However, after implementing God's financial principles, as per Schedule B, they had a surplus of $500 per month! Praise God! To achieve this, they reduced their overall expenses by $1,450 per month. This allowed them to increase their giving by $250 per month, raising it to 10 per cent (which is the biblical guideline for tithing, not a legalistic requirement).

QUESTION #5

What other expenses could Jim and Jennifer reduce?

TOM'S COMMENT

The following would help Jim and Jennifer reduce their expenses even further:

- Lower heating costs by ensuring the house is adequately insulated.
- Be conscious of utility costs, like turning out lights, taking shorter showers, or hanging laundry out to dry.
- Eliminate long-distance telephone calls by utilizing the internet when practical.
- Pay their mortgage weekly or biweekly instead of monthly to reduce interest costs.
- Drive their car only when necessary to minimize gas and maintenance costs. Use public transit when practical.

Please note, there are plenty of creative ways to reduce debt. Come up with some ideas by brainstorming on your own or with others.

QUESTION #6

What other cost-saving ideas would help Jim and Jennifer reduce their debt load?

TOM'S COMMENT

Jim and Jennifer should increase their income as they are able and apply their surplus to debt reduction, except for the first fruits, which should be sown into God's work.

In the beginning, it would have made sense for them to obtain a loan at a lower interest rate to pay off their credit cards. But they would need to understand that debt restructuring would only reduce their interest costs, not solve their financial problems. Their priority should be to ensure they spend less than they earn and use their surplus cash to pay down debt.

Furthermore, Jim and Jennifer could share their budget figures with a Christian who knows God's word on finances to obtain biblically based financial advice.

QUESTION #7

What is the relevance and application of the following verses regarding Jim and Jennifer's situation? Please discuss and write your comments below.

"Keep your lives free from the love of money and be content with what you have, because God has said, 'Never will I leave you; never will I forsake you'" (Hebrews 13:5).

TOM'S COMMENT

Initially, Jim and Jennifer were not content with God's provision as they spent more than they earned. However, once they learned and implemented God's financial principles, God enabled them to be content with a reduced lifestyle—within His provision and will for them.

"Your statutes are my delight; they are my counselors" (Psalm 119:24).

TOM'S COMMENT

Jim and Jennifer were blessed when they followed God's counsel and directives in His word concerning their finances.

"Your word is a lamp for my feet, a light on my path" (Psalm 119:105).

TOM'S COMMENT

Jim and Jennifer studied God's word, and God, through His word, directed them.

"Be sure you know the condition of your flocks, give careful attention to your herds" (Proverbs 27:23).

TOM'S COMMENT

Once Jim and Jennifer tracked their expenses and developed and implemented a budget, they understood their financial condition. They no longer needed to make financial decisions based on guesswork. Instead, they could base their financial decisions on their financial facts.

11. Case Study #2: A Single Man Learns and Applies Biblical Financial Principles

Ron is a single man who recently became a Christian. A friend introduced him to the Christian Financial Concepts ministry headed by Larry Burkett. Ron listened to some of Burkett's tapes and read several of his books, including books written by Howard

Dayton and Ron Blue. All three authors focused on teaching the biblical principles of financial management. Ron was astonished to learn that God's word, the Bible, contained so much wisdom on finances!

Although he was a new Christian, he sensed God directing him to start his own business. This was unsettling, and it made Ron nervous because he had few customers and owed a lot of money. Nevertheless, he obeyed God's directive for his life and started his own business.

As Ron worked hard at building his business, he diligently studied God's word on finances. In prayer, he asked the Lord several times to help him implement biblical principles in his personal *and* business finances.

As a result, he came to understand that God discouraged debt and that God's best for His children was to be debt-free (Deuteronomy 28:1–44). Having learned this, Ron committed to paying off all his debt as quickly as possible.

However, Ron also realized that God directs His followers to give to His work and that the minimum biblical guideline in Scripture is 10 per cent of your income (Matthew 23:23). As Ron continued to study God's word on finances, he realized he had a "dual responsibility" as a Christian. He was responsible for paying off all his debt and giving God the first fruits (Proverbs 3:9–10).

Initially, Ron felt he could not afford to give to God's work because of his debt load. Nevertheless, he meditated on key Scriptures related to debt and giving for several months. Afterward, in sheer faith, he started giving 10 per cent to his church despite his debt. This wasn't easy because his income was modest, and the business's cash flow was tight.

Notwithstanding, God honored Ron's faith, obedience, and sacrificial giving by blessing his business way beyond his imagination! Ron's business prospered, and within three years, he owned a business that would normally take the average entrepreneur twenty years to build! For example, customers came from sources that Ron never imagined and in ways that clearly indicated they were a blessing from God, not because of his hard work. Also, Ron paid off all of his debt within that same period, including his mortgage. He was debt-free! Ron frequently thanked God for his newly acquired wisdom in his personal and business finances.

Ron purposely continued to live a middle-class lifestyle, and as God blessed his business, he increased his giving. Today, Ron and his wife continue to study and diligently apply God's financial principles. As a result, they enjoy being debt-free and having the privilege to give generously—generally about 50 per cent of their income. Consider Jesus's words in Luke 12:48: "From everyone who has been given much, much will be demanded; and from the one who has been entrusted with much, much more will be asked."

It is important to remember that as your income increases, raise your standard of giving, not your standard of living!

QUESTION #1
What do you think had the most significant impact on Ron in changing his way of thinking about debt, giving, and managing money in general?

TOM'S COMMENT

Ron studied and meditated upon God's word on finances by listening to Larry Burkett's resources and books and other biblically based financial books by Howard Dayton and Ron Blue. These books are loaded with Scriptures that relate to finances, such as Romans 12:2 and Joshua 1:8.

Ron's testimony illustrates God's ability to accomplish what He desires through His word. Isaiah 55:11 reminds us: "So is my word that goes out from my mouth: It will not return to me empty, but will accomplish what I desire and achieve the purpose for which I sent it."

QUESTION #2

When Christians are in debt, should they focus on paying off debt and defer giving to God's work until they are debt-free? Or is it essential to give regularly to God's work even when in debt? Please explain your answer.

TOM'S COMMENT

Giving God the first fruits demonstrates your faith and trust in Him (Proverbs 3:5–6, 9–10). As mentioned, God discourages debt (Proverbs 22:7), and it is God's best for people to be debt-free as per Deuteronomy 28:1–12.

Christians should make debt reduction and repayment a priority, but not at the expense of robbing God. Malachi 3:8, 10 describes God's position on withholding money entrusted to us:

> "Will a mere mortal rob God? Yet you rob me. But you ask, 'How are we robbing you?' In tithes and offerings …

Bring the whole tithe into the storehouse, that there may be food in my house. Test me in this," says the LORD Almighty, "and see if I will not throw open the floodgates of heaven and pour out so much blessing that there will not be room enough to store it."

Please understand that we are no longer under Mosaic law but grace because of what Christ accomplished on the cross. Therefore, giving a minimum of 10 per cent is not a matter of legalism. However, it is an important guideline, and I believe it is the minimum amount a successful business person should give.

In summary, a Christian has a dual responsibility to pay down debt as quickly as possible and to give to God's work. It's not one or the other!

QUESTION #3

In the Bible, God demonstrated His awesome ability to give supernaturally because He is all-powerful, all-knowing, and omnipresent. What are some biblical examples of God providing miraculously for His people financially or materially?

TOM'S COMMENT

Here are a few of the many examples in the Bible of God's supernatural provision.

- In 1 Chronicles 29, God provided all the materials needed for the building of the temple. Of interest, there is no indication they incurred any debt. God blessed *miraculously,* and David praised the Lord in the presence of the assembly, acknowledging that it all came from God's hand (see verses 11–14).

- God used Elisha to *miraculously* provide a surplus of oil to the widow so that she could pay off all her debt (2 Kings 4:1–7).
- Jesus Christ *miraculously* fed five thousand people with five loaves of bread and two fish (Mark 6:37–44).
- God provided the Israelites with food (fresh manna) every day in the desert (Exodus 16).

QUESTION #4

In light of God's awesome power evidenced by the miracles He performed in the Bible, is it unrealistic for Christians with significant debt to give to God's work while also paying down their debt? Why or why not?

TOM'S COMMENT

It is not unrealistic for a Christian with even substantial debt to give generously to God's work while paying down their debt! God encourages and rewards generosity in 2 Corinthians 9:6–7:

> Whoever sows sparingly will also reap sparingly, and whoever sows generously will also reap generously. Each of you should give what you have decided in your heart to give, not reluctantly or under compulsion, for God loves a cheerful giver.

QUESTION #5

Discuss what is the relevance and application of the following verses concerning Ron's situation. Write your comments below each verse:

"Honor the LORD with your wealth, with the firstfruits of all your crops; then your barns will be filled to overflowing, and your vats will brim over with new wine" (Proverbs 3:9–10).

TOM'S COMMENT

Ron honored the Lord with his wealth by giving the first 10 per cent to God's work, even though he had a lot of debt initially and a small business with limited cash flow.

"If you fully obey the LORD your God and carefully follow all his commands I give you today ... The LORD will open the heavens, the storehouse of his bounty, to send rain on your land in season and to bless all the work of your hands. You will lend to many nations but will borrow from none" (Deuteronomy 28:1, 12).

TOM'S COMMENT

Ron fully obeyed God by implementing God's financial principles in his business and personal life. As a result, God did indeed open the heavens, the storehouse of His bounty, and blessed the work of Ron's hands with a substantial business and the ability to become debt-free within three years.

"A tithe of everything from the land, whether grain from the soil or fruit from the trees, belongs to the LORD; it is holy to the LORD" (Leviticus 27:30).

TOM'S COMMENT

Ron followed the biblical principle of giving the first 10 per cent of all his increase to God's work, even when he had significant debt and a tight cash flow. God blessed Ron's business because of his faith, obedience, and commitment to the Lord.

"Trust in the LORD with all your heart and lean not on your own understanding; in all your ways submit to him, and he will make your paths straight" (Proverbs 3:5–6).

TOM'S COMMENT

Ron learned and implemented God's financial principles and followed God's will, even when it didn't make sense from a natural, human perspective. Basically, Ron completely trusted God for the outcome.

"Keep this Book of the Law always on your lips; meditate on it day and night, so that you may be careful to do everything written in it. Then you will be prosperous and successful" (Joshua 1:8).

TOM'S COMMENT

Ron meditated on God's word and applied it to his personal and business life. As a result, God prospered him abundantly.

12. Case Study #3: Successful Business Owners Learn God's Way of Managing Money

Ken and Shirley are married with two children. They own a successful business and have above-average incomes. They had no problems obtaining credit with their high earnings as the bank was more than willing to lend them large sums of money. Additionally, they never worried about their debt load because they had always had sufficient income to service their debt in the past.

Unfortunately, the economy entered a severe recession, which caused the sales and profitability of their company to decline significantly. Consequently, they had no choice but to substantially reduce their salaries, which meant they could no longer pay their mortgage.

As a result, the financial institution holding their mortgage foreclosed on their home and sold it in the middle of a bad recession, at the worst time! Ken and Shirley were confused and could not understand why God would allow this to happen to them.

For the first time in a long time, Ken and Shirley spent quality time with the Lord each day in prayer. Specifically, they prayed that the bank would not put their business into bankruptcy. They asked God to direct them to someone who could help them.

In an unusual way, God led them to a godly accountant who understood how to apply God's financial principles to business and personal finances. The accountant recommended reading certain books by Larry Burkett, Ron Blue, and Howard Dayton and meditating upon specific Scriptures. The memorization of

Scriptures significantly changed Ken and Shirley's thinking on finances, and they grew spiritually.

Over several years, their accountant counseled and assisted them in applying biblical principles to their business and personal finances. As a result, they successfully developed and implemented a personal and corporate budget and moderated their personal lifestyle.

As well, although Ken and Shirley were Christians for many years, they started to give a minimum of 10 per cent of their income to God's work regularly for the first time. Because of their obedience to God's word, God sustained them and their business through the long recession.

When the recession ended, Ken and Shirley were determined to continue to manage their finances God's way and to become debt-free. Within six years, God blessed their business, and they were entirely free of debt, both personally and corporately!

Approximately ten years later, as a result of applying God's principles to their investments and all aspects of their personal and corporate finances, they retired with a comfortable standard of living.

Ken and Shirley saw this as a miraculous provision and blessing from God because, for some time, they believed they would never have sufficient assets to retire. Today, they serve the Lord in several ministries on a volunteer basis.

QUESTION #1

At the beginning, what biblical principles did Ken and Shirley violate? Please provide a reference to Scripture for each point.

TOM'S COMMENT
- They spent all their income and failed to save for future needs and emergencies (see Proverbs 21:20).
- They did not follow God's directive for minimal debt (see Deuteronomy 28:1–44; Proverbs 22:7).
- They did not honor God by giving their first fruits to His work (see Proverbs 3:9–10).
- They trusted in their business, rather than in God, to meet their needs (see Philippians 4:19).
- They did not habitually spend quality time with the Lord in prayer, and they made life decisions on their own (see John 15:5).
- They had no personal or corporate budget (see Luke 14:28–30).
- They did not seek the counsel of the Lord (see 1 Kings 22:5).
- They did not acknowledge God's ownership of their possessions (see Haggai 2:8).

QUESTION #2
What erroneous assumption did Ken and Shirley make at the beginning?

TOM'S COMMENT
Ken and Shirley assumed their above-average incomes from their successful business would continue. This is contrary to Scripture. One's level of income and business success is dependent on God's will (James 4:13–15; Proverbs 27:1).

QUESTION #3

In what ways did Ken and Shirley experience the truth of Proverbs 22:7, which says, "The rich rule over the poor, and the borrower is slave to the lender"?

TOM'S COMMENT

The bank foreclosed on their home and sold it at the worst possible time, during a nasty recession (see Proverbs 22:26–27). Hence, their excessive debt resulted in the loss of their home.

QUESTION #4

In the latter part of their business life, what biblical principles did Ken and Shirley follow? Please provide a Scripture reference for each point.

TOM'S COMMENT

- They spent quality time with the Lord each day in prayer (see 2 Chronicles 7:14).
- They asked God for His wisdom (see James 1:5) and His direction (see Psalm 32:8).
- They developed and implemented a budget, spent less than they earned, and used the surplus to pay down debt (see Proverbs 27:23).
- They made God a priority in their finances by tithing (see Malachi 3:8–10).

- They sought the counsel of the Lord in prayer (see 2 Chronicles 18:14).
- They followed biblical counsel from their accountant (see 1 Corinthians 2:14–15).
- They meditated upon and implemented God's word on finances (see Joshua 1:8).
- They learned to be content with a less lavish lifestyle (see Philippians 4:11–13).
- They made debt reduction a priority (see Proverbs 22:7).
- They trusted God to sustain them and their business through the harsh recession (see Isaiah 46:4).
- They renewed their minds (see Romans 12:2) in God's word (see Psalm 119:105).

QUESTION #5

Why does God allow His children to encounter financial difficulties? What greater purpose could God have in mind?

TOM'S COMMENT

God has a plan and purpose in every trial His children encounter. As noted in Romans 8:28, "We know that in all things God works for the good of those who love him, who have been called according to his purpose."

God's other intentions for allowing financial trials could be:

- To "prune" us (i.e., remove unfruitful ways of thinking and acting) so that we will bear more "fruit" (John 15:1–8).
- To draw us closer to the Lord (Matthew 11:28–30).

- To teach us to depend on Him and connect to Him (John 15:5).
- To develop perseverance and spiritual maturity (James 1:3–4).
- To nurture a deep faith and trust in the Lord (Proverbs 3:5–6).

QUESTION #6

What are the benefits of memorizing and meditating upon God's word?

TOM'S COMMENT

- To change how you think about money (Romans 12:1–2).
- To learn God's wisdom on finances in His word (2 Timothy 3:16–17).
- To believe in God's ways, not the world's ways (1 Corinthians 2:16).
- To follow God's will, not your own (Psalm 25:8–9).
- To understand Satan's financial deceptions (John 8:31–32).

QUESTION #7

What is the relevance and application of the following verses related to Ken and Shirley's situation? Discuss and write your comments below.

Now listen, you who say, "Today or tomorrow we will go to this or that city, spend a year there, carry on business and make money." Why, you do not even know what will happen tomorrow. What is your life? You are a mist that appears for a little while and then vanishes. Instead, you ought to say, "If it is the Lord's will, we will live and do this or that." (James 4:13–15)

TOM'S COMMENT

Ken and Shirley assumed their business would always be successful and provide them with above-average incomes. In the early part of their business life, they did not acknowledge that the success of their business depended on God's blessings. They likely felt they had everything under control. The biblical truth is that only God is in control (Psalm 103:19).

"Sacrifice thank offerings to God, fulfill your vows to the Most High, and call on me in the day of trouble; I will deliver you, and you will honor me" (Psalm 50:14–15).

TOM'S COMMENT

After Ken and Shirley lost their home, they called upon the Lord daily in prayer. God answered their prayers and sustained their business through the prolonged recession. For instance, their company did not go bankrupt, which was a real possibility, and it was their only income source.

"Do not conform to the pattern of this world, but be transformed by the renewing of your mind. Then you will be able to test and approve what God's will is—his good, pleasing and perfect will" (Romans 12:2).

TOM'S COMMENT

Ken and Shirley meditated upon and memorized God's word on finances. In this way, they "renewed their minds" and began to think in a godly fashion. As a result, they started making God-honoring financial decisions.

For example, they developed and implemented personal and corporate budgets to ensure they spent less than they earned. Then they applied the surplus to pay down debt and save for retirement. As well, they prioritized giving faithfully to God's work.

"Even to your old age and gray hairs I am he, I am he who will sustain you. I have made you and I will carry you; I will sustain you and I will rescue you" (Isaiah 46:4).

TOM'S COMMENT

God rescued Ken and Shirley from near financial disaster and supernaturally led and sustained them through the severe and prolonged recession.

QUESTION #8
What should you do if you are in financial difficulty?

TOM'S COMMENT
If you are in financial difficulty, I encourage you to meditate on Isaiah 46:4 daily and trust God to sustain you through this difficult time. God has a plan and a purpose in every trial He allows in the lives of His followers.

The truth is that God is in control of *all* our circumstances. Psalm 103:19 encourages us with these words, "The LORD has established His throne in the heavens, and His sovereignty rules over all" (NASB).

Sometimes God's purpose is to teach us vital lessons, like essential biblical principles, or to help us develop patience and perseverance (James 1:2–4). God will use our trials to draw us closer to Him and teach us to depend on Him (John 15) and to manage money His way.

Because of God's mercy and compassion toward us, His followers often experience spiritual growth and unexpected blessings during difficult times.

What should you *not* do if you are in financial difficulty?

TOM'S COMMENT
If you are facing financial hardship, *do not ignore the problem!* Don't rely on debt restructuring or borrowing more money, even

at a lower interest rate, thinking that you have solved your financial issues. Instead, study and meditate on biblical principles concerning finances, and apply them.

Time and time again, God's word is a tried and proven way to manage money effectively and pay down debt. There is no substitute for getting into His word, as it is through His word and His Spirit that God changes the way people think about and manage money (Romans 12:2; Joshua 1:8).

13. Case Study #4: The Financial Story of Mr. Borrower and Mr. Saver

This case study consists of two hypothetical but common individuals, Mr. Borrower and Mr. Saver, both whom I have seen multiple times over the past forty years. Unfortunately, many more people fall into Mr. Borrower's situation, and only a small percentage manage money like Mr. Saver.

14. Two Mortgages: Benefits of Paying Your Mortgage Down Faster

Mr. Borrower and Mr. Saver each borrow $500,000 to buy a home. They earn the same income. Their mortgage repayment is amortized over the same thirty-year period with an interest rate of 2.5 per cent per annum. Their required minimum monthly payment is $1,975.60. However, that is where the similarities end.

Mr. Saver applies biblical financial principles in managing money. He develops and implements a budget to ensure he spends less than he earns each month, which gives him a *surplus* to put towards his debt. In doing so, Mr. Saver consistently pays an extra $400 per month against his mortgage. As a result, his mortgage is paid off in twenty-three years and one month, with incurred interest charges of $158,765.

Mr. Borrower, on the other hand, does not see the priority of paying down his mortgage faster, so he pays the minimum amount requested by the bank. Instead, he decides to enjoy life more by spending any surplus funds, generally on wants and desires, not needs.

Consider the total payments, interest costs, and the number of payments made between Mr. Borrower and Mr. Saver in the following scenario. Mr. Borrower pays $1,975.60 per month, for thirty years, accumulating to a total of $711,218. Hence Mr. Borrower's total interest paid is $211,218. On the other hand, Mr. Saver pays $2,375.60 per month for twenty-three years, accumulating to a total of $658,765. Hence in total, Mr. Saver pays $158,765 of interest. Therefore, Mr. Saver saves about $52,453 (calculated as $211,218 less $158,765 which equals $52,453).

In addition, Mr. Saver is debt-free after twenty-three years! He then takes his former mortgage payment of $2,375.60 and invests it in a balanced portfolio that provides him with a return of about 6 per cent per annum over the next six years and eleven months.

At this point, Mr. Saver has approximately $247,238 for retirement. At the same time, Mr. Borrower has just paid off his mortgage and needs to start saving for retirement.

A key Scripture that applies here is Proverbs 21:20, which states, "The wise man saves for the future, but the foolish man spends whatever he gets" (TLB). By sacrificing along the way and exercising patience, self-control, and discipline, Mr. Saver is tremendously better off than Mr. Borrower, specifically by $247,238! This is because Mr. Saver has *compound interest* working in his favor.

Unfortunately, Mr. Borrower carries his debt for too long, does not prioritize paying down his debt, and ends up worse off financially.

When you review the above numbers, it becomes crystal clear as to why God discourages debt! It's no secret that financial institutions make a ton of money from people who take their time to pay off their debts.

Regrettably, that money could be used to benefit you or your family. But, more significantly, it could be invested into God's kingdom to reap eternal rewards (Matthew 16:27).

Further, in the Parable of the Tower (Luke 14:28–30), Christ admonished us to plan ahead. You can see that Mr. Saver planned well ahead for the long term. As a result, he was much better off financially than Mr. Borrower.

The previous example with a fixed mortgage rate of 2.5 per cent would have been applicable as of early 2022. However, at the time of writing this book, the spring of 2022, interest rates around the world have started to increase very significantly. Where they will end up no human being knows; only God knows. However, I can say this: if interest rates increase, the amount of money that can be saved by paying down your mortgage quickly is even greater than the example provided above.

For example, let's use the same assumptions—that Mr. Borrower and Mr. Saver each have mortgages of $500,000, except that the interest rate is 5 per cent. The regular monthly payment that Mr. Borrower would make would be $2,684.11 per month for total payments of $966,278 over the thirty years.

And let's assume similarly that Mr. Saver pays an additional $400 per month— $3,084.11. Mr. Saver will be debt-free within twenty-two years and seven months, incurring total interest costs of $834,805.

As can be seen, Mr. Saver is better off by $131,473 (i.e., $966,278 less $834,805). So as interest rates increase, the amount that Mr. Saver can save is even greater as he's paying down his principal faster.

And to be consistent with the previous example, assume that Mr. Saver takes his $3,084.11 per month and invests it for seven years and five months at a return of 6 per cent. After thirty years, Mr. Saver would have $349,463 for retirement, whereas Mr. Borrower would only be debt-free. As you can see, with interest rates at 5 per cent, Mr. Saver is better off by $349,463 while if the mortgage rate was at 2.5 per cent, Mr. Saver is better off by $247,238. Clearly, as interest rates go up, the individual who follows the biblical financial principles in paying down their mortgage quickly will be even better off!

Sadly, I could share the many times I've seen people spend all their regular income during their lifetime. When they entered retirement, they still had a mortgage, car loan, credit card debt, or a line of credit.

Since they did not follow the biblical admonition to plan and save for future needs, they suffered the consequences later. Such suffering comes in the form of financial stress, forced downsizing of one's home and lifestyle, inability to help children or grandchildren with their education, and having to work to service debt even if faced with health issues and stress.

On the other hand, I've also seen thousands of cases where God's people have followed His way of managing money. When they reached their later years, they were totally debt-free. They had saved up a significant amount for retirement and were living comfortably with no financial worries or related stress.

15. Summary: Benefits of Debt Reduction

I can provide many stories of people who studied and implemented God's financial principles and became totally debt-free. Over forty years, I have taught millions of people about the dangers of debt and the importance of working towards a debt-free lifestyle—about two million people hear my Financial Moment teachings every week on radio and television!

As a result, I've been privileged to witness thousands of individuals and couples totally eliminate their debt, and see thousands reduce their debt considerably. Praise God!

Of interest, not one person has ever regretted becoming debt-free. No one has ever said, "Hey Tom, we miss those mortgage payments" or "We wish we had those two car loan payments." Instead, everyone who has paid off their debt has expressed gratitude for having the financial stress eliminated from their lives. In addition, couples are always thankful for restored marital relationships due to debt elimination.

I sincerely believe that if you ask the Lord in faith for wisdom (James 1:5) and specific direction (Psalm 25:12), He will take you on a personal journey with Him towards financial healing.

Further, if you are willing to be content to live within God's provision (even a little less so you have a surplus to pay down debt and save for future needs), then the God of the universe will give you His peace and bless you financially. In John 14:27, Jesus said: "Peace I leave with you; my peace I give you. I do not give to you as the world gives. Do not let your hearts be troubled and do not be afraid."

Further, God will give you the perseverance you need to become debt-free if you ask Him in faith and yoke yourself with Him to complete the task. I am reminded of Jesus's invitation in Matthew 11:28–30:

> "Come to me, all you who are weary and burdened, and I will give you rest. Take my yoke upon you and learn from me, for I am gentle and humble in heart, and you will find rest for your souls. For my yoke is easy and my burden is light."

Are you willing to yoke yourself with God to manage the money He has entrusted to you? Are you ready to surrender your financial situation to Him, trusting He can teach you and equip you to become debt-free? If yes, your financial future will be brighter and more promising!

16. Appendix to Chapter II: Jim and Jennifer's Budget

Jim and Jennifer's Financial Situation Before Implementing God's Financial Principles		
REVENUES FOR A TYPICAL MONTH		
Salary and Wages (net of tax withholdings)	Husband	$2,500
	Wife	$2,500
Investment Income		
Miscellaneous income		
Total projected revenue for a typical month		$5,000

Jim and Jennifer's Financial Situation Before Implementing God's Financial Principles (Schedule A)

		Total	Monthly Amount
1	House Maintenance	$1,800 /12 =	$150
2	Property Taxes	$3,000 /12 =	$250
3	House Insurance	$600 /12 =	$50
4	Auto Replacement	/60 =	$0
5	Auto Repairs & Maintenance	$1,800 /12 =	$150
6	Auto Insurance	$3,000 /12 =	$250
7	Vacation	$1,800 /12 =	$150
8	Investments (e.g. retirement & education)*	/12 =	$0
9	Health Care	$900 /12 =	$75
10	Gifts - Christmas and birthdays, etc.	$1,500 /12 =	$125
11	Other	$3,000 /12 =	$250
TOTAL NEEDED FOR NON-MONTHLY / IRREGULAR EXPENSES:			**$1,450**

Note the denominators above will depend upon the number of months from now until the expenses are incurred, therefore adjust the formula as necessary.

Prepare this form initially, and revise only when there are changes.

* If investments are paid monthly, then there is no need to record on Form 3 rather include on Form 5.

Jim and Jennifer's Financial Situation Before Implementing God's Financial Principles		
1 DONATIONS		**$250**
2 HOUSING		
Mortgage/rent	1,000	
Property Taxes	250	
Electricity	250	
Gas	200	
Water	50	
Phones, internet, cable	100	
Maintenance	150	
Insurance	50	
Total Housing:		**$2,050**
3 FOOD		**$700**
4 AUTOMOBILE		
Replacement	0	
Gas & Oil	400	
Insurance	250	
Maintenance	150	
Total Auto Expenses:		**$800**
5 DEBTS		
Credit cards	400	min payment
Loans-plc	100	min payment
Other		
Total Debt Service:		**$500**

6	ENTERTAINMENT & RECREATION	
	Eating out	250
	Vacation	150
	Sports/Gym	100
	Total Ent/Rec:	**$500**

7	CLOTHING	$350

8	INVESTMENTS (e.g. RRSP, RESP etc.)	$0

9	HEALTH CARE	$75

10	INSURANCE- LIFE & DISABILITY	$100

11	MISCELLANEOUS	
	Education	
	Gifts	125
	Other*	250
	Total Miscellaneous:	**$375**

TOTAL EXPENSES:	**$5,700**

TOTAL REVENUES (FORM 2):	**$5,000**

MONTHLY SURPLUS (DEFICIT):	**($700)**

* Miscellaneous-Other includes expenses that do not fit elsewhere, such as transit, allowances, toiletries, cosmetics, etc.

Schedule B

Jim and Jennifer's Financial Situation After Implementing God's Financial Principles		
REVENUES FOR A TYPICAL MONTH		
Salary and Wages (net of tax with-holdings)	Husband	$2,500
	Wife	$2,500
Investment Income		
Miscellaneous income		
Total projected revenue for a typical month		**$5,000**

Jim and Jennifer's Financial Situation After Implementing God's Financial Principles			Total		Monthly Amount
1	House Maintenance		$600	/12 =	$50
2	Property Taxes		$3,000	/12 =	$250
3	House Insurance		$600	/12 =	$50
4	Auto Replacement			/60 =	$0
5	Auto Repairs & Maintenance		$900	/12 =	$75
6	Auto Insurance		$1,500	/12 =	$125
7	Vacation		$600	/12 =	$50
8	Investments (e.g. retirement & education)*			/12 =	$0
9	Health Care		$900	/12 =	$75
10	Gifts - Christmas and birthdays, etc		$900	/12 =	$75
11	Other		$1,800	/12 =	$150
TOTAL NEEDED FOR NON-MONTHLY / IRREGULAR EXPENSES:					**$900**

Note the denominators above will depend upon the number of months from now until the expenses are incurred, therefore adjust the formula as necessary.

Prepare this form initially, and revise only when there are changes.

*If investments are paid monthly, then there is no need to record on Form 3 rather include on Form 5.

Jim and Jennifer's Financial Situation
After Implementing God's Financial Principles

1 DONATIONS		**$500**
2 HOUSING		
Mortgage/rent	1,000	
Property Taxes	250	
Electricity	250	
Gas	200	
Water	50	
Phones, internet, cable	100	
Maintenance	50	
Insurance	50	
Total Housing:		**$1,950**
3 FOOD		**$500**
4 AUTOMOBILE		
Replacement	0	
Gas & Oil	250	
Insurance	125	
Maintenance	75	
Total Auto Expenses:		**$450**
5 DEBTS		
Credit cards	400	min payment
Loans-plc	100	min payment
Other		
Total Debt Service:		**$500**

6	ENTERTAINMENT & RECREATION		
	Eating out	50	
	Vacation	50	
	Sports/Gym	0	
	Total Ent/Rec:		**$100**

7	CLOTHING		$100

8	INVESTMENTS (E.G. RETIREMENT & EDUCATION)		$0

9	HEALTH CARE		$75

10	INSURANCE- LIFE & DISABILITY		$100

11	MISCELLANEOUS		
	Education		
	Gifts	75	
	Other*	150	
	Total Miscellaneous:		**$225**

TOTAL EXPENSES:	**$4,500**

TOTAL REVENUES (FORM 2):	**$5,000**

MONTHLY SURPLUS (DEFICIT):	**$500**

* Miscellaneous-Other includes expenses that do not fit elsewhere, such as transit, allowances, toiletries, cosmetics, etc.

107

III

HOW TO DEVELOP AND IMPLEMENT A BUDGET

A. OBJECTIVE OF THIS CHAPTER

To learn how to develop and implement a budget.

B. KEY BIBLICAL PRINCIPLE

In many places throughout the Bible, God admonishes us to plan ahead. Planning your finances is best accomplished by using a budget. If you prefer, you can call it a spending plan or a cash flow plan.

1. The Purpose of Budgeting

The purpose of budgeting is to ensure you spend less than you earn, giving you a surplus each month. You can use this surplus to pay down debt or save for future needs, including unexpected expenditures.

About 90 per cent of people do not have a workable budget. The result is that most spend more than they earn and accumulate debt, not a surplus. As well, many make financial decisions based on guesswork or personal desires rather than financial facts.

A proper budgeting system will provide the financial facts needed to make wise decisions. I cannot overstate that making decisions based on guesswork and "gut feelings" is dangerous. God instructed His people, "Be sure you know the condition of your flocks, give careful attention to your herds" (Proverbs 27:23).

Remember that when Proverbs was written, most people were farmers, so the modern-day application of this biblical principle is that we need to understand where our money is going—like housing, automobile, and food expenses, as well as other categories. In other words, *it is essential to track your expenses.*

Further, you need to understand your assets and liabilities. An asset is something you can sell, turn into cash, and use to pay off some of your debts. A liability is money you owe, including but not limited to credit cards, personal lines of credit, automobile loans, a mortgage, property taxes, income taxes, utilities, medical and dental bills, as well as personal loans owed to family or friends.

For your liabilities, you need to know the payment terms, interest rates, and renewal dates on your mortgage or loans. Remember, the bank prefers you extend your amortization period on your mortgage as long as possible. However, if you pay your mortgage off in a shorter period, you will save thousands of dollars in interest!

Understanding your income streams and sources is also vital to determine if you are accumulating debt by spending more than you earn. Or are you spending less than you earn and producing a surplus to pay off debt and save for future needs?

In over four decades of giving biblically based financial advice, I can confidently say that nine out of ten people do not manage their monthly cash flow well because they have not tracked their expenses or created a workable budget.

Unfortunately, many are unaware that their debt situation is gradually worsening. Developing and implementing a proper budgeting system will provide the financial facts needed to make *prudent financial decisions.* Proverbs 21:5 states, "The plans of the diligent lead to profit as surely as haste leads to poverty."

Developing and implementing a budget is consistent with biblical principles. For example, in the Parable of the Tower (Luke 14:28–30), Jesus Christ warned us to plan. In fact, Jesus considered it foolish to have no plan. A budget is an excellent tool that, when used correctly, can help you plan your finances effectively.

There are a variety of budgeting systems available. Some are quite detailed, provide extensive information, and take considerable time to understand and maintain. Others are straightforward, simpler to learn, and require less maintenance each month.

In 1982, I developed the Copland Budgeting System, which I have used in my accounting firm and financial ministry to help individuals and couples with their personal finances. This budgeting system provides sufficient details and is simple to learn and maintain with a minimal time commitment.

In addition, because it is an Excel-based system, anyone with a basic understanding of Excel can customize the template to their preference. And the price is right! You can download the budgeting system at no cost from our website. Visit us at www.coplandfinancialministries.org. A thirty-minute video also explains how to use the Copland Budgeting System.

Using any other budgeting system is acceptable, providing it allows you to track all your expenses, balance your budget, and compare your actual expenses to your budget each month. Of course, the budgeting system you choose needs to track your liabilities as well.

Most importantly, whatever budgeting system you choose, make sure you follow it diligently. Ultimately, it should provide you with the financial facts so that you can make wise, biblically based financial decisions.

If you invest the time to learn and implement a sound budgeting system, the benefits will far outweigh the time and sacrifice it takes to maintain it in the long run.

2. The Copland Budgeting System Overview of Forms

The following explains the Copland Budgeting System. Again, you can download it at no cost from our website as an Excel data file. A blank hard copy is also available at the end of this chapter for those who cannot access the internet or do not have Excel software on their computer.

These are the forms for the Copland Budgeting System in the Excel data file:

Form #1: Assets and Liabilities
Form #2: Revenues for a Typical Month
Form #3: Non-Monthly Expense Planning
Form #4: Savings Account Allocations
Form #5: Estimated Monthly Budget—Types of Expenses in Each Category
Form #6: Actual Expenses and Revenues
Form #7: Budget Analysis

For ease of calculation on the budgeting forms, please round all figures to the nearest dollar.

3. Step 1: List Your Assets and Liabilities on Form #1

Assess your current financial position by listing your assets and liabilities on form #1 (Proverbs 27:23). Include all debts, as some can be easily missed, such as personal loans from friends or relatives, overdue property taxes or income taxes, and dental or medical bills. It is always best to face the reality of your financial situation up front, even if it is initially discouraging. Remember, for ease of calculation, round all figures to the nearest dollar.

4. Step 2: List Your Revenues on Form #2

Use form #2 to summarize your income. Record your salary or wages, minus any income tax withholdings and other deductions. The program should transfer your total revenues to the bottom of form #5, Estimated Monthly Budget, to calculate your monthly surplus or deficit.

5. Step 3: Plan for Non-Monthly Expenses on Form #3

Many expenses do not arise monthly, such as gifts, vacations, annual insurance premiums, repairs, maintenance, or entertainment costs. As a result, they are often overlooked when developing a budget.

To ensure adequate cash is available for these non-monthly expenses as they arise, it is important to set aside the necessary funds throughout the year. Otherwise, you may be forced to take on debt to cover these non-monthly expenses. For example, if you plan to spend $1,200 on vacation a year from now, you would be wise to save $100 per month. This will ensure you can pay for your holiday and avoid having to put it on credit, then likely struggle to pay it off.

There are also non-monthly expenses, like house maintenance and car repairs, that must be estimated for the year and included in form #3. Again, it is imperative to allocate these funds each month, perhaps in a savings account.

While it is impossible to predict exactly what those costs will be in any given year, you can make a decent estimate and save a reasonable amount each month to cover these costs. As an example, for the average used car, about $100 per month is sufficient to cover most repairs and maintenance. So, on form #3, you would enter $1,200. The Copland budgeting template will automatically divide this amount by 12, reflecting the $100 on form #5. Next, complete form #3 for the other non-monthly, irregular expenses and include a long-term projection regarding the replacement of your automobile.

For instance, suppose you plan to replace your vehicle in five years (sixty months), and you want to buy a quality used car for around $12,000, then you should put $200 per month into your savings account to have the cash to purchase your next automobile. This is calculated as $12,000 divided by 60 = $200 per month.

6. Step 4: Transfer Funds from Chequing Account to Savings Account on Form #4

In general, a significant amount is needed to save every month for non-monthly expenses. Therefore, transfer the total amount shown on form #3 for non-monthly expenses into your savings account each month, and "earmark" the amount on form #4 according to the corresponding expense category. The program will automatically transfer the amounts on form #3 to form #4 on the first of each month, assuming you have sufficient funds in your chequing account.

Let's suppose you are paid twice per month and do not have sufficient cash in your chequing account. In that case, you will need to transfer half of the amounts calculated on form #3 from your chequing account to your savings account each time you receive your pay cheque. If this applies, you could override the formulas (click on tools - protection - unprotect sheet) and input the exact numbers or change the formulas on form #4 by multiplying by 0.5, assuming you are comfortable with the Excel software.

Besides recording and transferring these amounts from form #3 to form #4, *be sure to move the equivalent amount of money from your checking account into your savings account*!

Additionally, when you incur non-monthly expenses, transfer the funds from your savings account into your chequing account to pay the bills. Remember to reduce the right expense category on form #4, as funds are withdrawn from your savings account. The program will automatically record the transfers from your savings account to your chequing account on forms #4 and #6, respectively.

The balance shown at the bottom of form #4 should show the portion of your savings account designated for a particular expense category. The aim is to identify how much of your savings account balance will be necessary for non-monthly expenses to avoid inadvertently spending these funds. Ultimately, the savings account figure shown on form #4 should agree with your savings account bank balance. If not, an entry may have been missed, requiring you to recheck your work.

It has been my experience over the years that many people accumulate savings in their savings account, like $2,000, and think it's okay to spend it. For example, suppose they consider purchasing a $400 item not explicitly designated within the "Savings Account Allocations" on form #4. It would be a mistake for them to think they can afford the $400 when the entire $2,000 has been set aside for *future expenses* they haven't incurred yet. In other words, *it would not be feasible* for them to spend the $400, even though they have it in their savings account. To be clear, the only funds allocated for "non-budgetary expenses" are those reserved as "Undesignated Funds" at the bottom of form #4.

7. Step 5: Estimate Where Your Money Is Being Spent on Form #5

The "non-monthly expense items" calculated on form #3 should transfer automatically to form #5. In the next step, estimate your current level of spending in each blank category on form #5. The program should calculate your monthly surplus or deficit on the bottom right.

If you have a deficit, then rework your budget by reducing your discretionary spending until your budget balances. If this is not possible, *either increase your income, or reduce other costs to balance your budget.* Be sure to *spend less than you earn each month*, and *use the surplus to pay off debt and save for future needs.*

Please go to our website to find a nine-minute video demonstration explaining the three most common budgeting errors people make, as follows:

The first common mistake people make when planning a budget is failing to factor in all their non-monthly expenses. This error leads to the impression that they have a surplus each month. However, upon entering all their non-monthly expenses, they actually have a deficit! Unfortunately, this oversight is all too common.

The second budgeting mistake demonstrated in the video occurs when a couple runs a negative cash flow because they spend more than they earn. However, they create a positive cash flow by cutting back on discretionary spending and increasing their income, which allows them to generate a positive cash flow and therefore pay down debt. In this situation, they are fortunate not to have to make a major downsizing decision.

Thirdly, we see how a couple incurred so much debt that even after increasing their income to the max and reducing their discretionary expenses as much as practical, they were still forced to downsize their home.

Visit our website www.coplandfinancialministries.org to access these videos. Across the top, click on budgeting and then scroll down a bit to the video which is titled "Initial budget, typical budget, budget where downsizing is necessary".

8. Step 6: Regularly Track Your Expenditures and Revenues on Form #6

Many people have a reasonable income level but spend more than they earn. In the long run, this can lead to financial difficulties and is often a major cause of conflict between couples.

Having served thousands of clients as a chartered professional accountant and financial adviser, I can affirm that most people are unaware of where their money is going. Consequently, they are prone to making poor financial decisions that negatively affect their finances in the long term.

Developing and implementing a budget is essential to gaining control of your finances. You can also refer to a budget as a "spending plan" or a "cash flow plan," as they are essentially the same. To accomplish this, you need to record all your expenses on form #6 to know where your money is being spent. Recording your expenses can be simplified if you follow these guidelines:

• I recommend a husband and wife use a joint chequing account to deposit their pay cheques. Almost all banks offer online access to your bank accounts and credit cards, so you can download your banking information at least monthly and keep track of your finances. If you pay for any items or services with cash, make sure you fill out form #6 to document where those funds were spent.

- Establish a joint savings account and earmark its funds per form #4.
- When you get your credit card statement each month, and presumably pay it in full, summarize your expenses (some credit card companies will do this for you). Then enter those amounts on form #6, whether paid by cash, cheque, or debit or credit card, in the designated column for each expense category. The total amount incurred and paid will reduce your chequing account balance. This step is unnecessary if you record your individual credit card charges each day, as stated below.
- On form #6, you can record your expenses on a monthly basis as suggested in point 1 through online banking, or you can record your daily expenses on the same form as you incur them. Be sure to note whether you paid by cash, cheque, debit card, or credit card. Round all figures to the nearest dollar, and if you forget the exact amount, record your best estimate. If you can track all your monthly expenses within $100, you are doing much better than most people.
- Record each transfer to and from your savings account into the appropriate column on form #6, and ensure that they agree with the corresponding transfers on form #4.

9. Step 7: Budget Analysis on Form #7

Using form #7, compare your actual expenses with your budget, and identify any overruns. Then prepare a new budget for the next month on form #5 with the necessary adjustments (with a new Excel data file). Budgets are subject to change over time, and a workable budget usually takes four to six months to develop, revise, and implement. So please don't get discouraged if you find the initial process challenging.

After balancing your monthly expenses and revenues for three to four months, set some longer-term financial goals, like debt reduction, retirement planning, saving for children's education, or replacing your automobile. Of course, you should always adjust your monthly budget to meet your financial goals.

Whenever you make a significant financial commitment, such as saving for an automobile, you may find it helpful to open a separate savings account, which can be done quickly online. In fact, some people have several savings accounts—one each for car replacement, annual insurance premiums, next year's vacation, and future roof replacement.

If, for example, you expect you will need to replace the roof of your house in six years at a cost of $6,000, set aside $1,000 per year or $84 per month to ensure you can afford the replacement when needed. This can be calculated on form #3 as "$6,000 divided by 72 equals $84 per month."

10. Starting a New Month

Once the current month is completed, save the Excel data file and label it for the month that just ended (e.g., "January Budget"). Next, get a blank copy of the budgeting template and label it with the current month (e.g., "February Budget").

Follow the steps outlined above, but note the following changes to the second and subsequent months.

1. If the numbers have not changed, it can be faster to "copy and paste" specific figures (such as annual non-monthly expense amounts on form #3) rather than inputting them again. Take care not to override any formulas.

2. Be sure to input the final balance from the previous month on form #4 into the current month's "Balance Forward— Prior Month" row so that you have the cumulative totals for your savings account.
3. Adjust the estimated budget on form #5 for the current month to conform to the "new monthly budget" on form #7 from the previous month.
4. You can now enter your daily expenses on form #6 on the current month's data file.

11. Year-to-Date Figures

If preferred, you can take a blank copy of the budgeting template and save it as "year-to-date for the upcoming year." Then enter your total expenses and revenue for the first month on the first line of form #6, then the total expenses and revenue for the second month on the second line of form #6, and so on.

Then enter the appropriate amounts on forms #2 and #5. Be sure to prorate based on the number of months that have passed since the beginning of the year. As an example, if you have a summary of six months' worth of expenses, be sure to divide the total expenses and revenues by six to arrive at the average monthly amount to reflect on forms #2 and #5.

If, however, you have only completed form #6 for the first four months of the year, then you would divide all of those amounts by four and put them in appropriate places on form #2 (i.e., your income) and form #5 (i.e., your expenses).

12. Final Points

Over time, accumulate a "cushion of cash" (I recommend six to nine months' worth of expenses) above the "earmarked savings" in your savings account (form #4 of the Copland Budgeting System).

This cushion will provide some financial security in the event of an unforeseeable financial hardship, such as a spouse losing their job or unexpected expenses (see Proverbs 21:20).

Once you have accomplished this, you will no longer need to prepare forms #3 and #4 each month. Also, since forms #1 and #2 only need updating for any monthly changes, you will only need to prepare forms #5, #6, and #7 each month as long as the balance in your savings account is maintained.

Please note that this system can help you project your new budget if you are considering a major purchase, such as a new house, or if you plan to retire. The goal is to determine whether you can afford the house or afford to retire.

Essentially, planning is a biblical principle that leads to success. Proverbs 21:5 states, "The plans of the diligent lead to profit as surely as haste leads to poverty."

13. In Summary

The Excel-based budgeting system provides a simple and organized way to *manage your monthly cash flow*. The above instructions are intended to help people track and manage their finances.

If you feel overwhelmed, remember that God is the greatest financial manager and accountant of all! With His help, you can gain control of your finances and be free from worry and anxiety (John 14:27).

Furthermore, if you faithfully follow God's biblical principles of financial management, He will also lead you out of debt. Keep in mind that "all things are possible with God" (Mark 10:27).

If you have questions, please contact info@biblefinance.org, and a financial coach affiliated with Copland Financial Ministries or I will get back to you. As a ministry, we offer biblically based financial advice at no cost.

C. HOW TO CHANGE THE WAY YOU MANAGE MONEY

Most Christians and non-Christians alike do not manage money God's way. Rather, they violate biblical financial principles and manage money the world's way, often unknowingly.

The most important step you can take to transform your money management mindset is to *study and meditate on God's word*. Romans 12:2 says, "Do not conform to the pattern of this world, but be transformed by the renewing of your mind." And how do you renew your mind? Joshua 1:8 gives the answer: "Keep this Book of the Law always on your lips; meditate on it day and night, so that you may be careful to do everything written in it. Then you will be prosperous and successful."

It would be beneficial to meditate on the following Scripture on a regular basis. Allow God to speak to you through his word and to change how you think about and manage money. Luke 14:28–30:

> "Suppose one of you wants to build a tower. Won't you first sit down and estimate the cost to see if you have enough money to complete it? For if you lay the foundation and are not able to finish it, everyone who sees it will ridicule you, saying, 'This person began to build and wasn't able to finish.'"

14. Assignment

Preparing your budget is the most important task you have! If you are married, make sure you include your spouse in the process.

If you do not currently use a budgeting system, consider the Copland Budgeting System which is available at no charge from our website www.coplandfinancialministries.org. Again, a thirty-minute video on the website explains how to use it.

If you encounter any difficulties developing a budget, send your questions to our email address info@Biblefinance.org. One of our financial coaches can assist you in developing a budget at no charge.

I encourage you to be not just a "hearer of the word" but also a "doer of the word" (James 1:22). Therefore, make the commitment to follow through and prepare a budget, or spending plan, if you prefer. Track your expenses diligently going forward and compare them to your budget each month.

Finally, review your budget to find areas where you can cut spending and increase income to create a positive cash flow each month. If you do this consistently, you will progress financially by paying down debt and saving for future needs.

15. Ideas to Reduce Expenses

To balance your budget, it's often necessary to reduce your spending. On form #5, you will find some suggestions for reducing expenses in various categories. I encourage you to *prayerfully* go through this list and ask the Lord to direct you to the practical ones you and your spouse can implement.

16. Mortgage Costs

Paying off your mortgage faster is an excellent way to save money in the long run. You can accomplish this by simply making additional payments against your mortgage, assuming you have the flexibility in your mortgage agreement. You certainly do not want to incur any significant penalties from the bank if you pay your mortgage off too early or too quickly.

Also, when your mortgage comes up for renewal, negotiate terms that allow you to pay it down faster. For example, certain mortgage agreements allow borrowers to double their payments. Others allow additional lump sum payments of up to 20 per cent per year of the principal without incurring penalties.

Again, speak to your bank or check your mortgage agreement for details. Generally, you do not want to incur major penalties for early payments, as these are typically very expensive!

Another way to save money is to pay your mortgage on a weekly or biweekly basis. As a result, you will pay off your mortgage earlier and save considerable interest over the long term.

17. Utility Costs

Another cost-saving strategy is to minimize utility costs as much as possible. Among other things, remember to turn off lights, do chores requiring electricity during off-peak hours, set your thermostat a couple of degrees lower to conserve energy, seal windows and doors properly to prevent heat loss, and stay on top of repairs and maintenance.

Also, consider swapping services with others instead of paying for repairs, maintenance, or renovations. Not only will these measures save you money, but they will also benefit the environment.

18. Shared Accommodation

If possible, consider sharing accommodation with another individual or family. In this way, you can reduce your overall expenses significantly, which will help you balance your budget. Any additional income could pay down debt and save for future needs.

This principle applies whether you rent or own. For instance, if you rent a house for $2,000 per month with a housemate, your monthly costs will be reduced by $1,000. That's a significant saving!

On the other hand, if you plan to purchase a condo or house, assuming you can afford it, you have two options:

1. You could buy a house or condo and rent a portion to a tenant. The rental income would help offset some costs of homeownership.
2. A second option is to purchase a home with someone else (or another family) to have joint ownership. Assuming it's a 50/50 equity ownership, you would only be responsible for half the mortgage, utilities, maintenance, repairs, property taxes, and insurance, and you could live in the house!

In today's high-cost housing market, sharing a home with another individual or family is a good financial decision, if practical.

19. Advantages of Shared Accommodation

The major advantage of shared accommodation is that people can significantly reduce their mortgage payments, utility costs, repairs and maintenance, insurance, and property taxes, often by 50 per cent!

In addition, you may enjoy the companionship of a housemate, particularly if you're single. Finally, there is the added benefit of safety when two people live together rather than alone.

Ecclesiastes 4:9–10, 12 states:

Two are better than one, because they have a good return for their labor: If either of them falls down, one can help the other up. But pity anyone who falls and has no one to help them up … Though one may be overpowered, two can defend themselves. A cord of three strands is not quickly broken.

20. Challenges of Shared Accommodation

Think of some challenges or disadvantages of sharing accommodation, and write your thoughts below before reading my comments. Readers often suggest ideas I hadn't thought about!

TOM'S COMMENT

As someone who has advised people about their finances for decades, I have seen many cases where shared accommodation has worked out well and saved people a lot of money. As a result, people have been able to get control of their finances.

On the other hand, the downside of shared accommodation is that it can pose significant challenges. As an example, if a housemate fails to pay their share of the costs, the entire expense may fall on you, causing financial stress and tension between you and your housemate.

In addition, even if your housemate is a family member or close friend, some people cannot live together because of differences in lifestyle, habits, values, personalities, likes, dislikes, and so forth.

QUESTION #1

What steps should you consider before entering a shared accommodation arrangement with someone? Please write your answers below, citing Scripture, if possible, then review my notes.

TOM'S COMMENT

Before you commit to sharing accommodation with a single person or multiple people, I recommend you review this checklist and consider the following:

- Develop a budget (Luke 14:28–30) with respect to the projected costs of the accommodation, including non-monthly expenses to see if you and your potential housemate can afford it.
- Assess your potential housemate's financial management skills (or lack thereof). Requesting a credit report is a good idea. If their credit history is poor with no reasonable explanation, avoid sharing accommodation with them.
- Determine their income level, debts and liabilities, current budget, and spending habits. As a rule, most people don't feel comfortable asking or answering questions of this nature. Nevertheless, if your potential housemate were to rent elsewhere or apply for a mortgage, they would have to disclose similar information to a landlord or bank.
- All parties need to track every expense related to the accommodation and provide receipts.
- Consider whether the lifestyle of your potential housemate is compatible with yours. Also, if you have children, how will the living arrangement affect them?

- Create a household emergency fund together for unexpected expenses (Proverbs 21:20).
- If you purchase a house together, discuss and agree on savings for significant future repairs and maintenance (Proverbs 21:5).
- Discuss up front what will happen if your housemate moves out (perhaps to marry). If you rent or own a place together, what will happen to the lease or mortgage agreement?
- Prepare a written contract between yourselves for clarity and to prevent forgetfulness about the terms of the deal. It should be simple, thorough, and address all possible scenarios. In most cases, a lawyer is not necessary.
- Purchase a home if you can afford it and rent a part of it out to generate income or consider living with your parents for a season if practical.
- Pray and ask God to reveal anything relevant about a potential housemate that may cause problems.

To decide whether you should enter a shared housing agreement with a particular individual or individuals, seek God's wisdom and his specific direction. James 1:5–6, states: "If any of you lacks wisdom, you should ask God, who gives generously to all without finding fault, and it will be given to you. But when you ask, you must believe and not doubt." And in Psalm 32:8, God promised: "I will instruct you and teach you in the way you should go; I will counsel you with my loving eye on you."

Be encouraged that as you meditate on God's word and seek His will, He will lead you to make the right decision concerning a potential housemate. Psalm 119:105 states, "Your word is a lamp for my feet, a light on my path." As you seek the Lord for guidance, ask in prayer if there is anything about a potential housemate that you should know before making a commitment to a shared accommodation arrangement.

Further, in Jeremiah 33:3, God's invitation is to "call to me and I will answer you and tell you great and unsearchable things you do not know."

Hence, pray and ask God to reveal those unsearchable things to you that may not be obvious, so you can make a wise decision up front.

QUESTION #2

Is it acceptable to share accommodation with a non-believer? Give some thought and prayer to this question. Please provide your answer with a reference to Scripture, if possible.

TOM'S COMMENT

I recommend you consider what Paul said in 2 Corinthians 6:14–15, 17:

> Do not be yoked together with unbelievers. For what do righteousness and wickedness have in common? Or what fellowship can light have with darkness? What harmony is there between Christ and Belial? Or what does a believer have in common with an unbeliever? ... Therefore, "Come out from them and be separate," says the Lord.

QUESTION #3

Does the above Scripture apply to shared accommodation? In other words, will you be "unequally yoked" if your potential housemate is a non-believer? Please explain your answer below.

TOM'S COMMENT

It depends on the nature of the arrangement. If it's a short-term rental or a rental agreement that you can get out of easily, then you're probably not unequally yoked in a financial sense. However, if it's a long-term rental agreement, as with a condo or house purchase, then I believe you're yoked financially. It is generally not a good idea for a Christian to enter such an agreement with a non-believer in this situation.

These are merely guidelines, and to be sure, there is no substitute for praying and discerning what God's will is. In Ephesians 5:15–17, the Lord cautions: "Be very careful, then, how you live—not as unwise but as wise, making the most of every opportunity .... Do not be foolish, but understand what the Lord's will is."

Therefore, before making any significant decisions, it is critical to pray and ask God for his wisdom (James 1:5) and his specific direction (Psalm 25:12). You can avoid many hardships down the road, financial or otherwise, by waiting patiently on God.

QUESTION #4

Aside from accommodation costs, are there other expenses that can be shared with a housemate?

TOM'S COMMENT

Yes, housemates can share expenses in multiple ways. Here are a few examples, although this list is not exhaustive. There are also additional ideas on how to minimize your expenditures in general.

Vehicles: If you live with others, try to get by with one vehicle to save money on insurance and maintenance. You can also share the actual cost of the car. Whenever practical, use public transportation to save money on gas and minimize wear and tear on your vehicle.

Instead of trading in a new car every couple of years, keep it for its entire life, which can also save money. An alternative to buying new is to buy a good quality used car, reducing your overall cost.

Groceries: You can reduce your grocery bill in many ways, like sharing the cost of food when you live with others. You can also watch for sales and specials, plan meals to prevent food waste, freeze leftovers, and frequent farmer's markets, which has the added benefit of supporting your local economy!

Debts: Ensure that your credit card balance is paid off every month. Interest rates can be exorbitant if you run a positive balance. If you get into the position of not paying your balance, stop using your card and make paying it off a priority to avoid getting further into debt.

Dining Out: You can dine out occasionally, but this is one area where you can control your spending simply by not going out to eat. Instead, plan special meals at home, try new recipes, explore international cuisine, set your table Italian-style, and make eating at home fun!

Another area where people overspend is buying takeout coffee or tea. To save money, buy a container of coffee or tea and make it at home to take with you rather than visiting a coffee shop. You'd be surprised at how quickly miscellaneous expenses add up!

Remember the Lord's instruction in Proverbs 13:11: "Whoever gathers money little by little makes it grow." In other words, the emphasis in Scripture is to save a little at a time over a long period. For example, find the adventure in taking simple day trips, exploring local parks and trails, or simply converting your backyard into an enjoyable place to relax—at minimal expense, naturally!

Vacations: Instead of going on an expensive vacation, consider taking a "staycation." For example, find the adventure in taking simple day trips, exploring local parks and trails, or simply converting your backyard into a leisurely oasis, with minimal cost, of course!

Gym Memberships: Although gym memberships are purchased with the best of intentions, people rarely use them. Instead, consider other methods of exercising without spending money. As an alternative to paying for an expensive gym membership, walk, jog, or run regularly, and buy used equipment and weights to use at home.

Clothing: Shopping at thrift stores is an excellent way to save on clothing costs. If you prefer to buy new clothing, consider shopping at discount stores or only buying items on sale. Another option is to pass clothing down from an older sibling to a younger sibling or exchange clothing with friends who have similar-aged children.

Education: It's a good idea to save early for your children's education. By involving your children in this process, you can teach them valuable lessons about life and money.

For example, you can instruct them to save a portion of their allowance or earnings, such as 50 per cent for future education, 40 per cent for general savings and spending, and 10 per cent for the Lord's work.

Instilling biblical financial principles in your children at an early age will help them develop good money habits that will pay off for a lifetime.

Holidays and Gifts: Plan your Christmas shopping well in advance and purchase items throughout the year, preferably on sale, rather than waiting for the Christmas season when prices are higher. You may also want to agree with family and friends to limit the cost of your gifts.

Alternately, make homemade cards, treats, or holiday crafts, which can also be given as gifts. Often, these are the most treasured gifts of all!

You can also forgo the gifts altogether and instead donate to a favorite charity, or simply enjoy spending time together over the holidays.

Miscellaneous: Miscellaneous expenses are expenses that don't fit into any other category. Most people underestimate miscellaneous expenses to be modest when in reality they are much higher than expected. This is definitely an area where you can easily overspend.

Be cautious therefore when tracking your miscellaneous expenses, and remember that God has promised to meet our needs, not necessarily our wants and desires (Matthew 6:31–33). Runaway miscellaneous expenses can add up quickly and significantly affect your budget.

21. Creative Ways to Increase Income
Another way to maintain a healthy, balanced budget and positive cash flow is to increase your income. Among the many ideas that exist, here are a few you may wish to consider:

- Improve your education so you can earn a higher income.
- Consider part-time employment besides your regular work.
- Apply your natural talents and spiritual gifts to your workplace because your strengths may position you for promotions.

- If your skills and expertise are not being used at your current job, it may be time to find an alternate position or career path.
- Consider renting out a room or basement apartment to generate income if you have the space. However, be selective when choosing a tenant, because the wrong tenant could cause you many headaches as a landlord.
- Turn your long-time hobby into a money-making venture, such as photography, freelance writing, baking, landscaping, or crafting.
- Don't let your closets collect dust with unused clothing, toys your kids no longer play with, and other items! Sell them!
- You could make extra income by childminding or pet-sitting if you are a stay-at-home parent.

D. CASE STUDIES, QUESTIONS, TOM'S COMMENTS

22. Case Study #1: Learning to Budget

Bill and Barb are married with two children. They have made their first attempt at developing a budget, but they are bewildered. Their initial budget shows a surplus, but they have noticed that the balance on their credit cards has increased over the past year, not decreased.

Bill and Barb's initial and revised budgets are attached as an appendix at the end of this chapter.

QUESTION #1
Please review Bill and Barb's initial budget on form #5, found on the first page of the appendix to this chapter. Do you think their budget is complete?

TOM'S COMMENT
No, their budget is incomplete as several key expenses have not been accounted for.

QUESTION #2
What specific expense categories have Bill and Barb missed? Please list them.

TOM'S COMMENT
They neglected to mention their property taxes, house mainten-ance, house insurance, auto insurance, auto maintenance, and replacement, vacation, retirement savings (RRSPs), and chil-dren's education savings (RESPs) and investments.

QUESTION #3
What do all these expenses have in common?

TOM'S COMMENT

All these expenses occur irregularly and are not incurred monthly. However, these types of expenses must be provided for in one's budget.

QUESTION #4

If they had been using the Copland Budgeting System, what form # would have recorded these types of expenses?

TOM'S COMMENT

Form #3 of the Copland Budgeting System records "Non-Monthly Expense Planning."

Review Bill and Barb's revised budget on form #5, which follows their initial budget, and note the differences. The reality is that Bill and Barb spend more than they earn, as demonstrated by a monthly deficit.

QUESTION #5

What expense categories have Bill and Barb still not provided for (even in their revised budget) that could create additional financial problems in the long run? Please write your answer.

TOM'S COMMENT

The couple has failed to account for the replacement of their automobile, savings for debt reduction (i.e., allocating more than just minimum payments on their credit cards and loan), savings, and investments for retirement (RRSP), and their children's education (RESP).

QUESTION #6
What is the risk of not accounting for non-monthly expenses in your budget?

TOM'S COMMENT
There is a high risk of overlooking some significant expenses and making unwise financial decisions based on inaccurate information.

QUESTION #7
What kind of mistakes could arise?

TOM'S COMMENT
If you fail to save for non-monthly expenses, you will likely have to borrow money and go further into debt. For example, unless you saved in advance to replace your car, you will have to rely on a loan to replace it.

Another benefit of saving for your next car is that you will be in a better position to negotiate a lower price when you pay with cash.

As a rule, failing to put aside funds for non-monthly expenses increases the likelihood of spending more than you can afford.

Many are prone to spending the money in their accounts, even though it should be dedicated to non-monthly expenses.

Forms #3 and #4 of the Copland Budgeting System can be used to determine how much money needs to be allocated to each category.

23. Case Study #2: A Single Man with a High Income

Paul is a single man who earns a high income. He recently received a call from his banker informing him that he had exceeded his personal line of credit once again. Paul was baffled, since he had just increased his credit limit about six months ago.

He met with his banker, who provided all the documentation showing that Paul had spent that amount. He was surprised at how much he had spent in such a short period.

As a result, Paul applied for a credit limit increase for the fourth time in two years. In order to solve his financial problems, he took on a part-time job in addition to his full-time job. Unfortunately, he had to inform his pastor that he could no longer devote time to church ministry due to a lack of time.

QUESTION #1

What steps should Paul take to turn his financial situation around? Please list your ideas below in chronological order, and provide a reference to Scripture for each point.

TOM'S COMMENT

These are some of the main things Paul needs to do:

- Paul needs to develop and implement a budget (Luke 14:28–30) to ensure he spends less than he earns (Proverbs 21:20). He must track his expenses and know where his money is going (Proverbs 27:23).
- He must learn to be content with less in the way of material things (Philippians 4:11–13).
- He needs to learn and apply God's financial principles (2 Timothy 3:16). Participation in a small-group biblical financial study would be appropriate, such as my series "Financial Management God's Way."
- We offer many small groups on Zoom, so your location is not a problem. Go to www.coplandfinancialministries.org to learn more.
- He needs to obtain godly counsel before making any significant financial decisions (Psalm 1:1–3).
- He needs to prioritize his relationship with Jesus Christ rather than take on another job to support his current lifestyle at the expense of Christian ministry (Matthew 6:31–33). Instead, Paul must be willing to reduce his lifestyle to fit his financial means (1 Timothy 6:6–8).

QUESTION #2

Do you think that Paul's situation is common?

TOM'S COMMENT

Unfortunately, Paul's financial situation is all too common since it is too easy to obtain credit, allowing people to spend more than they earn.

QUESTION #3

Do you think that earning more income will solve Paul's financial problems? Write your answer below after considering the implications of Luke 16:10, where Jesus said: "The one who is faithful in a very little thing is also faithful in much, and the one who is unrighteous in a very little thing is also unrighteous in much" (NASB).

TOM'S COMMENT

Earning more money will not solve Paul's financial problems! Paul has not proven to be trustworthy in managing his present level of income. Because of this, Christ says he won't be trustworthy with handling more money.

In Matthew 25:14–30, the same biblical financial principle is in the Parable of the Talents. According to my experience, when people earn more money, they often go deeper into debt since banks and credit card companies lend even more money to higher-income earners.

QUESTION #4

Proverbs 21:20 (NRSV) states, "Precious treasure remains in the house of the wise, but the fool devours it." According to this proverb, which category does Paul fall into?

TOM'S COMMENT

It is evident that Paul falls into the *foolish* category because he spends everything he has, and beyond. He also neglects to save for future needs.

Discuss the relevance and application of the following verses concerning Paul's situation. Some verses indicate certain things Paul is not doing or should be doing. Write your comments below each verse.

"Commit to the LORD whatever you do, and he will establish your plans" (Proverbs 16:3).

TOM'S COMMENT

Paul must commit himself to accomplishing God's will in every area of his life, including his finances. If he does this, God has promised that his plans will succeed. Why? Because, in essence, those plans will be God's plans. Up to now, Paul has spent his money as he wished without consulting the Lord and following God's biblical principles.

"The plans of the diligent lead to profit as surely as haste leads to poverty" (Proverbs 21:5).

TOM'S COMMENT

Paul's decision to take a part-time job and resign from church ministry was hasty and made without thoughtful consideration, planning, or prayerfully seeking the Lord (1 Kings 22:5). According to Scripture, Paul seems more concerned about the temporal than the eternal. Colossians 3:1–2, tells us to "set your minds on things above, not on earthly things."

24. Case Study #3: Implementing a Biblically Based Budget

Dave and Debbie are married and have three daughters. They experienced a lot of financial difficulties when first married. After months of prayer and seeking God's wisdom and direction, they felt led to attend a small-group Bible study on God's principles of financial management.

They learned how to develop and implement a budget and record and track their expenses. Since then, they have diligently followed a budget and studied God's word about finances regularly to ensure they managed their money according to His will.

Their entire budget is outlined on forms #1–7 in the attached appendix. As indicated, they have accounted for and saved for all future anticipated expenses, including the replacement of their automobile, their children's education, and retirement.

Dave and Debbie also have an emergency savings account for unforeseen expenditures. They praised God for His wisdom since Dave had been out of work for months last year, and the couple had enough savings to meet all their needs.

Further, their only remaining debt is their mortgage. If they continue making additional payments on it, they will be totally debt-free within six years! They regularly thank God for giving them His wisdom and direction for their finances.

QUESTION #1
What steps did Dave and Debbie take that are consistent with God's word on finances? Please provide a Scripture reference as able.

TOM'S COMMENT
Some things Dave and Debbie did that are consistent with God's word:

- They learned and applied God's word on finances (see Joshua 1:8).
- They developed and implemented a budget (see Luke 14:28–30).
- They asked God for his wisdom and direction (see James 1:5).
- They praised God for his wisdom, direction, and blessings (see Psalm 150:1–6).
- They diligently applied biblical principles and followed through (see Proverbs 21:5).

- They managed their money God's way (see 1 Chronicles 29:11–13) and saved for the unexpected—like emergencies (see Proverbs 21:20).
- They made debt reduction a priority (see Proverbs 22:7).
- They saved for future needs (see Proverbs 21:20).
- They looked to God and His word for guidance, not the world (see Psalm 119:105).

QUESTION #2

Review Dave and Debbie's budget in the appendix at the end of this chapter. Then answer the question: Are Dave and Debbie in good financial shape?

TOM'S COMMENT

Dave and Debbie are in excellent financial shape because they have accounted for all types of expenses in their budget. In addition, they have applied biblical principles to their finances and are committed to managing money God's way.

QUESTION #3

How are the following verses relevant and applicable to Dave and Debbie's situation? Write your comments below:

"Be sure you know the condition of your flocks, give careful attention to your herds" (Proverbs 27:23).

TOM'S COMMENT

Dave and Debbie tracked and recorded their income, expenses, assets, and liabilities according to this proverb. As a result, they had a solid understanding of their financial situation, which enabled them to make wise decisions based on financial facts rather than guesswork or personal desires.

"For I know the plans I have for you," declares the LORD, "plans to prosper you and not to harm you, plans to give you hope and a future. Then you will call on me and come and pray to me, and I will listen to you. You will seek me and find me when you seek me with all your heart" (Jeremiah 29:11–13).

TOM'S COMMENT

In prayer, Dave and Debbie purposely sought God's will concerning their finances. God heard their prayers and directed them. As a result, they experienced God's peace and blessings.

"The plans of the diligent certainly lead to advantage, But everyone who is in a hurry certainly comes to poverty" (Proverbs 21:5 NASB).

TOM'S COMMENT

Dave and Debbie planned their finances diligently, which benefited them financially, emotionally (they had God's peace), and spiritually (they were doing God's will). They did not make impulsive decisions, and as a result, they reaped the benefits of managing God's money God's way.

"The wise man saves for the future, but the foolish man spends whatever he gets" (Proverbs 21:20, TLB).

TOM'S COMMENT

Dave and Debbie were wise because they saved for future needs. In Luke 14:28–30, Jesus instructed: "Suppose one of you wants to build a tower. Won't you first sit down and estimate the cost to see if you have enough money to complete it? For if you lay the foundation and are not able to finish it, everyone who sees it will ridicule you, saying, 'This person began to build and wasn't able to finish.'"

In the Parable of the Tower, Christ advised us to plan ahead. This is what Dave and Debbie did as they projected costs for their:

- Short-term needs, like non-monthly expenses.
- Intermediate needs, like debt reduction and car replacement.
- Long-term needs, like children's education and retirement.

Aside from that, they created an emergency fund for unforeseen expenditures to ensure they had sufficient funds when they arose.

"Let no debt remain outstanding, except the continuing debt to love one another, for whoever loves others has fulfilled the law" (Romans 13:8).

TOM'S COMMENT

Praise God! By paying all their debts when due, Dave and Debbie have been faithful and practical witnesses to their creditors.

25. Questions Regarding Budgeting

Please send an email to info@biblefinance.org with any questions you have about budgeting, and either I or one of our financial coaches will give you biblically based financial advice. You can also access many free resources on our website. Simply go to www.coplandfinancialministries.org.

I pray that the good Lord will give you wisdom (James 1:5) and direct you according to His will (Psalm 25:12) in how you manage the money God has entrusted to you (Haggai 2:8).

26. Appendix to Chapter III

Bill and Barb's Initial Budget	
1 DONATIONS	**$200**
2 HOUSING	
Mortgage/rent	900
Property Taxes	0
Electricity	200
Gas	150
Water	40
Phones, internet, cable	60
Maintenance	0
Insurance	0
Total Housing:	**$1,350**
3 FOOD	**$500**
4 AUTOMOBILE	
Replacement	0
Gas & Oil	250
Insurance	0
Maintenance	0
Total Auto Expenses:	**$250**
5 DEBTS	
Credit cards	300 min payment
Loans	100 min payment
Other	
Total Debt Service:	**$400**

6	ENTERTAINMENT & RECREATION	
	Eating out	200
	Vacation	0
	Sports/Gym	50
	Total Ent/Rec:	**$250**

7	CLOTHING	$100

8	INVESTMENTS (E.G. RETIREMENT & EDUCATION)	$0

9	HEALTH CARE	$50

10	INSURANCE- LIFE & DISABILITY	$100

11	MISCELLANEOUS	
	Education	
	Gifts	0
	Other*	0
	Total Miscellaneous:	**$0**

TOTAL EXPENSES:	**$3,200**

TOTAL REVENUES (FORM 2):	**$4,000**

MONTHLY SURPLUS (DEFICIT):	**$800**

* Miscellaneous-Other includes expenses that do not fit elsewhere, such as transit, allowances, toiletries, cosmetics, etc.

149

Bill and Barb's Revised Budget

1 DONATIONS		**$200**

2 HOUSING		
Mortgage/rent	900	
Property Taxes	233	
Electricity	200	
Gas	150	
Water	40	
Phones, internet, cable	60	
Maintenance	150	
Insurance	50	
Total Housing:		**$1,783**

3 FOOD		**$500**

4 AUTOMOBILE		
Replacement	0	
Gas & Oil	250	
Insurance	150	
Maintenance	150	
Total Auto Expenses:		**$550**

5 DEBTS		
Credit cards	300	min payment
Loans	100	min payment
Other		
Total Debt Service:		**$400**

6 ENTERTAINMENT & RECREATION	
Eating out	200
Vacation	100
Sports/Gym	50
Total Ent/Rec:	**$350**

7 CLOTHING	$100

8 INVESTMENTS (E.G. RETIREMENT & EDUCATION)	$0

9 HEALTH CARE	$100

10 INSURANCE- LIFE & DISABILITY	$100

11 MISCELLANEOUS	
Education	
Gifts	100
Other*	200
Total Miscellaneous:	**$300**

TOTAL EXPENSES:	**$4,383**

TOTAL REVENUES (FORM 2):	**$4,000**

MONTHLY SURPLUS (DEFICIT):	**($383)**

* Miscellaneous-Other includes expenses that do not fit elsewhere, such as transit, allowances, toiletries, cosmetics, etc.

Dave and Debbie
FORM # 1 - ASSETS AND LIABILITIES

ASSETS:		Estimated Current Value
1 Cash, chequing, and savings accounts		5,000
2 Investments - personal level		25,000
3 Real Estate	Principal residence	600,000
	Other	
4 Retirement savings		
	Husband	35,000
	Wife	35,000
5 Other Assets:		
TOTAL ASSETS:		**$700,000**

For practical reasons, do not list personal items that will likely never be sold (e.g. furniture, personal jewelry etc.)

LIABILITIES:	Interest Deductible Yes or No	Estimated Amount Owing
1 Credit cards		
2 Personal Loan(s) - parents		
3 Other Debts		
(a)		
(b)		
(c)		
4 Mortgage - principal residence	No	$75,000
Other		
5 Other Liabilities		
TOTAL LIABILITIES:		**$75,000**

TOTAL ASSETS	**$700,000**	
TOTAL LIABILITIES:	**- $75,000**	
	= NET WORTH	**$625,000**

FORM # 2 REVENUES FOR A TYPICAL MONTH FOR DAVE & DEBBIE		
Salary and Wages (net of tax withholdings)	Husband	$4,250
Debbie works part time.	Wife	$1,250
Investment Income		
Miscellaneous income		
Total projected revenue for a typical month		$5,500

FORM #3
NON-MONTHLY EXPENSE PLANNING
FOR DAVE AND DEBBIE

		Total		Monthly Amount
1	House Maintenance	$1,200	/12 =	$100
2	Property Taxes	$3,000	/12 =	$250
3	House Insurance	$600	/12 =	$50
4	Auto Replacement	$15,000	/60 =	$250
5	Auto Repairs & Maintenance	$1,800	/12 =	$150
6	Auto Insurance	$1,560	/12 =	$130
7	Vacation	$1,200	/12 =	$100
8	Investments (e.g. retirement & education)*	$0		$0
9	Health Care	$1,200	/12 =	$100
10	Gifts - Christmas and birthdays etc	$1,200	/12 =	$100
11	Other	$2,400	/12 =	$200

TOTAL NEEDED FOR NON-MONTHLY / IRREGULAR EXPENSES: **$1,430****

Note the denominators above will depend upon the number of months from now until the expenses are incurred, therefore adjust the formula as necessary.

Prepare this form initially, and revise only when there are changes.

*For Dave & Debbie - $500/month to retirement fund for last 8 years at 9% yields $70,952 today and $500 per month at 9% for another 25 years will provide over $1,200,000 for retirement.

Also $140 per month to education fund for 18 years at 9% provides over $75,000 - i.e. $25,000 per child

** one half i.e. $715 transfer from chequing to savings a/c on 1st and 15th -see form # 6

FORM #4 — SAVINGS ACCOUNT ALLOCATIONS FOR DAVE AND DEBBIE

Date	Receipts from Chequing a/c	Transfer to Chequing a/c	Balance	House Maintenance	Property taxes	House Insurance	Auto Replacement	Auto Repairs	Auto Insurance	Vacation	Investments	Health Care	Gifts	Other
1	715	0	715	50	125	25	125	75	65	50	0	0	50	100
2		0	715											
3		-100	615	-100										
4		0	615											
5		0	615											
6		0	615											
7		0	615											
8		0	615											
9		-200	415											-200
10		0	415											
11		0	415											
12		0	415											
13		0	415											
14		0	415											
15	715	-250	880		-250									
16		0	880	50	125	25	125	75	65	50	0	50	50	100
17		0	880											
18		0	880											
19		0	880											
20		0	880											
21		0	880											
22		0	880											
23		0	880											
24		0	880											
25		-150	730					-150						
26		0	730											
27		0	730											
28		0	730											
29		0	730											
30		-100	630									-100		
31		0	630											
	1,430	-800		0	0	50	250	0	130	100	0	0	100	0

Funds in saving account	$630
Total designated funds	$630
Undesignated funds	$0

FORM # 5
DAVE AND DEBBIE'S BUDGET

1 DONATIONS		$550

2 HOUSING		
Mortgage/rent	1,242 **	
Property Taxes	250	
Electricity	200	
Gas	150	
Water	40	
Phones, internet, cable	60	
Maintenance	100	
Insurance	50	
Total Housing:		**$2,092**

3 FOOD		$500

4 AUTOMOBILE		
Replacement	250	
Gas & Oil	250	
Insurance	130	
Maintenance	150	
Total Auto Expenses:		**$780**

5 DEBTS		
Credit cards		
Loans		
Other		
Total Debt Service:		**$0**

6	ENTERTAINMENT & RECREATION		
	Eating out	50	
	Vacation	100	
	Sports/Gym	50	
	Total Ent/Rec:		**$200**
7	CLOTHING		$100
8	INVESTMENTS (E.G. RETIREMENT & EDUCATION)		$640
9	HEALTH CARE		$100
10	INSURANCE- LIFE & DISABILITY		$100
11	MISCELLANEOUS		
	Education incl in investments		
	Gifts	100	
	Other*	200	
	Total Miscellaneous:		**$300**
	TOTAL EXPENSES:		**$5,362**
	TOTAL REVENUES (FORM 2):		**$5,500**
	MONTHLY SURPLUS (DEFICIT):		**$138**

* Miscellaneous-Other includes expenses that do not fit elsewhere, such as transit, allowances, toiletries, cosmetics, etc.

** Mortgage will be paid off in 6 years

FORM # 6 — ACTUAL EXPENSES AND REVENUES FOR DAVE AND DEBBIE

Date	Balance	Receipt fr. saving a/c	Trf to saving a/c	Revenue	Donations	House	Food	Auto	Debts	E&R	Clothes	Investments	Health care	Life & disability Insurance	Misc.
1	$1,935	$0	$715	$2,750										$100	
2	$1,660	$0			$275										
3	$1,660	$100				$100									
4	$1,660	$0													
5	$1,410	$0					$250								
6	$1,410	$0													
7	$1,410	$0													
8	$1,410	$0													
9	$1,410	$200													$200
10	$1,410	$0													
11	$1,360	$0								$50					
12	$1,360	$0													
13	$1,360	$0													
14	$1,360	$0													
15	$2,403	$250	$715	$2,750	$275	$1,242									
16	$1,488	$0										$640			
17	$1,238	$0				$250	$250								
18	$913	$0								$75					
19	$913	$0													
20	$713	$0				$200									
21	$563	$0									$150				
22	$413	$0				$150									
23	$373	$0				$40									
24	$313	$0				$60									
25	$313	$150						$150							
26	$313	$0													
27	$63	$0						$250							
28	$63	$0													
29	$63	$0													
30	$13	$100								$50			$100		
31	$13	$0													
		$800	$1,430	$5,500	$550	$2,042	$500	$400	$0	$175	$150	$640	$100	$100	$200

ROUNDING TO NEAREST DOLLAR ON ALL FORMS SHOULD HELP SIMPLIFY YOUR WORK

FORM # 7
BUDGET ANALYSIS FOR DAVE AND DEBBIE

		Present Budget (Form #5)	Actual Revenue Expense (Form # 6)	Difference + or -	New Monthly Budget
	EXPENSES				
1	Donations	$550	$550	$0	
2	Housing	$2,092	$2,042	$50	
3	Food	$500	$500	$0	
4	Auto	$780	$400	$380	
5	Debts	$0	$0	$0	
6	Ent. & Rec.	$200	$175	$25	
7	Clothes	$100	$150	-$50	
8	Investments (e.g. RRSP, RESP)	$640	$640	$0	
9	Health care	$100	$100	$0	
10	Insurance - Life & disability	$100	$100	$0	
11	Misc.	$300	$200	$100	
	Total Expenses:	**$5,362**	**$4,857**	**$505**	**$0**

		Present Budget (Form #2)	Actual Revenue Expense (Form # 6)	Difference + or -	New Monthly Budget
	REVENUES	**$5,500**	**$5,500**	**$0**	
	REVENUES LESS EXPENSES				
	SURPLUS (DEFICIT)	**$138**	**$643**	**$505**	

COPLAND BUDGETING SYSTEM
FORM # 1 - ASSETS AND LIABILITIES

ASSETS		Estimated Current Value
1	Cash, chequing, and savings accounts	
2	Investments - personal level	
3	Real Estate Principal residence	
	Other	
4	RRSPs	
	Husband	
	Wife	
5	Other Assets:	
TOTAL ASSETS:		**$0**

For practical reasons, do not list personal items that will likely never be sold (e.g. furniture, personal jewelry etc.)

LIABILITIES:	Interest Deductble Yes or No	Estimated Amount Owing
1 Credit cards		
2 Personal Loan(s)		
3 Other Debts		
(a)		
(b)		
(c)		
4 Mortgage - principal residence		
Other		
5 Other Liabilities		
TOTAL LIABILITIES:		**$0**

TOTAL ASSETS:	**$0**	
TOTAL LIABILITIES:	-$0	
	=NET WORTH	**$0**

Go to www.Coplandfinancialministries.org to learn regarding Copland budgeting system. And watch the 30 minutes of video that explain how to use the system. If you would like a print out of all forms, click on file-print-entire workbook - OK.

FORM # 2 REVENUES FOR A TYPICAL MONTH		
Salary and Wages (net of tax withholdings)	**Husband**	
	Wife	
Investment Income		
Miscellaneous income		
Total projected revenue for a typical month		**$0**

FORM #3
NON-MONTHLY EXPENSE PLANNING

		Total	Monthly Amount
1	House Maintenance	/12 =	$0
2	Property Taxes	/12 =	$0
3	House Insurance	/12 =	$0
4	Auto Replacement	/60 =	$0
5	Auto Repairs & Maintenance	/12 =	$0
6	Auto Insurance	/12 =	$0
7	Vacation	/12 =	$0
8	Investments (e.g. retirement & kids education) *	/12 =	$0
9	Health Care	/12 =	$0
10	Gifts - Christmas and birthdays, etc.	/12 =	$0
11	Other	/12 =	$0
TOTAL $ NEEDED FOR NON-MONTHLY / IRREGULAR EXPENSES:			**$0**

Note the denominators above will depend upon the number of months from now until the expenses are incurred, therefore adjust the formula as necessary.

Prepare this form initially, and revise only when there are changes.

* If saving for retirement in children's education is paid monthly then just include the appropriate figure on Form #5.

FORM #4 — SAVINGS ACCOUNT ALLOCATIONS

Date	Receipts from Chequing a/c	Transfer to Chequing a/c	Balance	House Mainte-nance	Property taxes	House Insurance	Auto Replace-ment	Auto Repairs	Auto In-surance	Vaca-tion	Invest-ments	Health Care	Gifts	Oth-er
BALANCE FWD				0	0	0	0	0	0	0	0	0	0	0
1	0		0	0	0	0	0	0	0	0	0	0	0	0
2	0	0	0											
3	0	0	0											
4	0	0	0											
5	0	0	0											
6	0	0	0											
7	0	0	0											
8	0	0	0											
9	0	0	0											
10	0	0	0											
11	0	0	0											
12	0	0	0											
13	0	0	0											
14	0	0	0											
15	0	0	0											
16	0	0	0											
17	0	0	0											
18	0	0	0											
19	0	0	0											
20	0	0	0											
21	0	0	0											
22	0	0	0											
23	0	0	0											
24	0	0	0											
25	0	0	0											
26	0	0	0											
27	0	0	0											
28	0	0	0											
29	0	0	0											
30	0	0	0											
31	0	0	0											
Funds in saving account				$0	0	0	0	0	0	0	0	0	0	0
Total designated funds				0										
Undesignated funds				$0										

FORM # 5
ESTIMATED MONTHLY BUDGET
TYPES OF EXPENSES WITHIN EACH CATEGORY

1	DONATIONS	

2	HOUSING	
	Mortgage/rent	
	Property Taxes	0
	Electricity	
	Gas	
	Water	
	Phones, internet, cable	
	Maintenance	0
	Insurance	0
	Total Housing:	**$0**

3	FOOD	

4	AUTOMOBILE	
	Replacement	0
	Gas & Oil	
	Insurance	0
	Maintenance	0
	Total Auto Expenses:	**$0**

5	DEBTS	
	Credit cards	
	Loans	
	Other	
	Total Debt Service:	**$0**

6	**ENTERTAINMENT & RECREATION**		
	Eating out		
	Vacation	0	
	Sports/Gym		
	Total Ent/Rec:		**$0**
7	**CLOTHING**		
8	**INVESTMENTS (E.G. RETIREMENT & KIDS EDUCATION)**		**$0**
9	**HEALTH CARE**		**$0**
10	**INSURANCE- LIFE & DISABILITY**		
11	**MISCELLANEOUS**		
	Education/Child care		
	Gifts	0	
	Other*	0	
	Total Miscellaneous		**$0**
	TOTAL EXPENSES:		**$0**
	TOTAL REVENUES (FORM 2):		**$0**
	MONTHLY SURPLUS (DEFICIT):		**$0**

* Miscellaneous-Other includes expenses that do not fit elsewhere, such as transit, allowances, toiletries, cosmetics, dry cleaning, books/magazines, household supplies, etc.
Please only fill in the boxes highlighted in grey - everything else is generated automatically.
PLEASE FOLLOW THIS INSTRUCTION TO AVOID MESSING UP THE FORMULAS.

FORM # 6— ACTUAL EXPENSES AND REVENUES

Date	Balance	Receipt fr. saving a/c	Trf to saving a/c	Revenue	Dona-tions	House	Food	Auto	Debts	E&R	Clothes	Invest-ments	Health care	Life & disability Insur-ance	Misc.
	$0														
1	$0	$0													
2	$0	$0													
3	$0	$0													
4	$0	$0													
5	$0	$0													
6	$0	$0													
7	$0	$0													
8	$0	$0													
9	$0	$0													
10	$0	$0													
11	$0	$0													
12	$0	$0													
13	$0	$0													
14	$0	$0													
15	$0	$0													
16	$0	$0													
17	$0	$0													
18	$0	$0													
19	$0	$0													
20	$0	$0													
21	$0	$0													
22	$0	$0													
23	$0	$0													
24	$0	$0													
25	$0	$0													
26	$0	$0													
27	$0	$0													
28	$0	$0													
29	$0	$0													
30	$0	$0													
31	$0	$0													
		$0	$0	$0	$0	$0	$0	$0	$0	$0	$0	$0	$0	$0	$0

ROUNDING TO NEAREST DOLLAR ON ALL FORMS SHOULD HELP SIMPLIFY YOUR WORK

FORM # 7
BUDGET ANALYSIS

	Present Budget (Form #5)	Actual Expense (Form # 6)	Difference + or -	New Monthly Budget
EXPENSES				
1 Donations	$0	$0	$0	
2 Housing	$0	$0	$0	
3 Food	$0	$0	$0	
4 Auto	$0	$0	$0	
5 Debts	$0	$0	$0	
6 Ent. & Rec.	$0	$0	$0	
7 Clothes	$0	$0	$0	
8 Investments (e.g. RRSP, RESP)	$0	$0	$0	
9 Health care	$0	$0	$0	
10 Insurance - Life & disability	$0	$0	$0	
11 Misc.	$0	$0	$0	
Total Expenses:	**$0**	**$0**	**$0**	**$0**
	Present Budget (Form #2)	**Actual revenue (Form # 6)**	**Difference + or -**	**New Monthly Budget**
REVENUES	**$0**	**$0**	**$0**	
REVENUES LESS EXPENSES				
SURPLUS (DEFICIT)	**$0**	**$0**	**$0**	**$0**

This budgeting template was developed by Tom Copland as a ministry to help people manage their personal finances. To learn more please visit www.coplandfinancialministries.org

IV

QUESTIONS TO CONSIDER BEFORE BORROWING OR CO-SIGNING

A. CHECKLIST OF QUESTIONS

People often borrow money or co-sign a loan without reviewing the biblical principles related to borrowing or co-signing. Consequently, they later encounter difficulties because they have not followed God's financial principles. If you are contemplating borrowing money, I strongly recommend you work through the following eight questions. At the very least, read them thoroughly to better understand the biblical prerequisites that should be met before you borrow or co-sign a loan. It will be helpful to refer to this checklist in the future.

1. Do You Have a Plan, Such as a Budget?

Do you have a plan, such as a budget, to ensure you can comfortably afford the loan payments?

In the Parable of the Tower in Luke 14:28–30, Jesus Christ admonished us to plan ahead. And Proverbs 21:5 says, "The plans of the diligent lead to profit as surely as haste leads to poverty."

When you consider borrowing, be sure to include all related costs in your budget with regard to the item you plan to purchase (like repairs, insurance, and maintenance, as applicable). It is critical to prepare your budget *before* making the commitment to buy and borrow, to ensure that you can afford the loan payments. As Proverbs 16:3 states, "Commit to the Lord whatever you do, and he will establish your plans."

2. Do You Understand Your Responsibility to Pay Your Debts on Time?

In light of Psalm 37:21, do you understand that it is your responsibility to repay the entire loan and to make your payments on time?

What kind of "light in a world of darkness" are Christians who do not pay their debts on time? In Matthew 5:16, Jesus said, "In the same way, let your light shine before others, that they may see your good deeds and glorify your Father in heaven."

3. Have You Prayed and Given God the Opportunity to Provide the Funds?

Have you prayed for a reasonable amount of time and given God an opportunity to provide the funds in a way that glorifies Him?

People often buy things hastily because credit is too readily available. Consequently, they miss out on *God's unique provision.* Remember, God loves to bless His children as well as meet their needs.

The apostle Paul wrote in Philippians 4:19, "My God will meet all your needs according to the riches of his glory in Christ Jesus." Note that God promises to meet your needs, not "God and the bank" or "God and the credit card company" but the Lord Himself will meet *all of your needs as you put Him first.*

The Lord comforts us in Matthew 6:31–33 with these words:

"So do not worry, saying, 'What shall we eat?' or 'What shall we drink?' or 'What shall we wear?' For the pagans run after all these things, and your heavenly Father knows that you need them. But seek first his kingdom and his righteousness, and all these things will be given to you as well."

4. Have You Given God the Opportunity to Provide at a Lower Cost or an Alternative?

Have you given God the opportunity to provide what you need at a lower cost or perhaps to provide an alternative? People may lean in the right direction with respect to a particular purchase, but they haven't prayed and allowed God to provide them with a better deal, so they miss out on His blessings.

Always pray before making any major purchase or taking on any significant debt. Ask the Lord for His wisdom, as only God knows the future (Isaiah 46:10), and only He has control (Psalm 103:19). Several times daily, I pray the following Scripture from James 1:5: "If any of you lacks wisdom, you should ask God, who gives generously to all without finding fault, and it will be given to you." We all lack wisdom because we are imperfect beings.

Since none of us can predict the future and only God knows, there is no substitute for prayer and asking God for His wisdom and direction. And as you pray, be sure to listen to what the Lord has to say. In John 10:27, Jesus said, "My sheep listen to my voice; I know them, and they follow me." God can communicate with you in a variety of ways. For example, the Holy Spirit can highlight a Scripture (Psalm 119:105), give you a sense of peace or lack of peace about a particular situation (John 14:27), or speak to you through a godly adviser (Proverbs 15:22).

5. Could It Be That God Does Not Want You to Have What You Are Asking For?

Have you considered that God simply may *not* want you to have what you are asking for? Sometimes, it is God's best for us to forgo the purchase of a particular material thing.

In Matthew 16:24–25, Jesus told his disciples: "Whoever wants to be my disciple must deny themselves and take up their cross and follow me. For whoever wants to save their life will lose it, but whoever loses their life for me will find it."

It's important to be content to live within the limits of God's provision for you. In Luke 3:14, John the Baptist said, "Be content with your pay."

6. Is the Item You Plan to Purchase a Necessity?

Is the item that you plan to purchase *really* a necessity? Can you manage without it?

God has promised to meet our needs (Matthew 6:31–33) but not necessarily our wants and desires. Sometimes, God will bless us with things we don't really need, but we must be sure they are from Him and according to His will.

If you are thinking about purchasing something that is a want rather than a necessity, then the Lord can provide the funds so that you won't have to borrow to get something you don't actually need. I personally believe that God will often provide the cash if He wants you to buy anything that is a "want or desire" as opposed to a need.

7. Have You Prayed for God's Guidance?

Have you and your spouse, if married, prayed sincerely for God's guidance? Do you have God's peace about this potential expense?

If you have prayed, do both of you (Genesis 2:24, "one flesh") have God's peace about borrowing the money or purchasing the item? In John 14:26–27, Jesus said:

> "The Advocate, the Holy Spirit, whom the Father will send in my name, *will teach you all things* and will remind you of everything I have said to you. *Peace I leave with you;*

my peace I give you. I do not give to you as the world gives. Do not let your hearts be troubled and do not be afraid." (Emphasis added.)

The Holy Spirit can provide peace or lack of peace before you make a decision about a proposed purchase or borrowing money.

8. Have You Spent Sufficient Time in Prayer Seeking God's Direction?

Finally, and most importantly, have you spent sufficient time in prayer with the Lord, seeking his specific direction concerning any important financial decisions you face?

Isaiah 48:17 says, "I am the LORD your God, who teaches you what is best for you, who directs you in the way you should go." If you haven't already done so, I recommend you keep a spiritual journal that documents your prayer requests and conversations with the Lord.

You may find it helpful to record what you sense God saying to you. Before you borrow money or make any major financial decision, check your journal for consistency from the Lord.

If you're considering taking on substantial debt for a major purchase, take your time, perhaps even months, and do not rush into it. According to Psalm 37:7, we should "be still before the LORD and wait patiently for him."

It is encouraging to know that the Lord has a plan for each of His children, including a plan for major life decisions, such as borrowing money. According to Jeremiah 29:11–14, God is involved in every aspect of our lives, including our finances. God says:

"I know the plans I have for you," declares the LORD, "plans to prosper you and not to harm you, plans to give you hope and a future. Then you will call on me and come and pray to me, and I will listen to you. You will seek me and find me when you seek me with all your heart. I will be found by you," declares the LORD.

God often directs us during the planning stage, so it's vital to seek His will, study His word, and listen to what He has to say *before* making any significant financial decisions. By asking God for guidance through these steps, we can avoid unnecessary financial hardship.

Therefore, it's essential to spend time in prayer with the Lord during the planning stage before borrowing money or making any major purchases. In this way, you will be sure to follow God's plan for your life.

If you have carefully considered each question, you are on the right path to accurately discern God's will regarding your financial decision. I personally believe that if you can sincerely say "yes" to all eight questions, then it's likely God's will is for you to borrow the money. Nevertheless, as explained in earlier chapters, it is best that you pay off all your debt first as soon as possible.

B. CASE STUDIES, QUESTIONS, TOM'S COMMENTS

9. Case Study #1: A Couple Engages in Biblical Planning Before Purchasing a Home

Ralph and Deborah have been married for seven years. They took part in our in-depth study, "Financial Management God's Way." Both had considerable debt from post-secondary education, so they followed Christ's advice to plan ahead (Luke 14:28–30). They created and followed a budget, spent less than they earned, and used their surplus funds to pay off debt, which took about two years.

During the study, one Scripture that God spoke to them through was Proverbs 21:20: "The wise man saves for the future, but the foolish man spends whatever he gets" (TLB). In response, they minimized their expenses and maximized their income, generating a monthly surplus, which allowed them to save for a decent down payment for a home within five years.

Originally, they wanted a four-bedroom house on a large lot with a two-car garage. They prayed and asked God for guidance. As they prepared their budget based on the cash flow projections for owning such a house, God revealed they could not afford it. Ralph and Deborah chose to be content with a smaller, more affordable home. At first, they were not sure what to do, and they knew they had to address other questions such as:

1. What was the maximum mortgage they could afford and still have a cushion within their monthly cash flow for unanticipated expenditures?
2. If they bought a house, what would be a reasonable estimate for property taxes, utilities, repairs, maintenance, and insurance? As part of their plan to purchase a house, they accounted for these costs in their budget.
3. Another key question was what neighborhood did God want them to live in?

Throughout the process of saving and planning to purchase their home, Ralph and Deborah fervently prayed and asked God for his wisdom (James 1:5) and His specific direction every step of the way (Psalm 32:8). They kept spiritual journals that tracked their prayer requests and God's communication to them through His word and Spirit.

Interestingly, as they compared notes, they both sensed the Lord was leading them to purchase a modest, affordable, semi-detached home. They made sure they had a reasonable surplus in their projected monthly budget for unexpected expenses.

In the initial stages of planning to buy a house, Ralph and Deborah were concerned because the price of houses had risen significantly in their area over the past few years. Their realtor encouraged them to buy a house as soon as possible, even if it meant taking out a large mortgage, since they believed houses would always continue to appreciate in value. Thankfully, Ralph and Deborah did not act impulsively. Instead, they sought the advice of a godly adviser who was independent of the realtors. The financial adviser reminded them that no one can predict the future (Proverbs 27:1), only God knows the future (Isaiah 46:10), and God is in control (Psalm 103:19). Ralph and Deborah, therefore, decided to "Be still before the Lᴏʀᴅ and wait patiently for him" (Psalm 37:7), and to trust God to provide a home for them when they had a sufficient down payment (Proverbs 3:5–6).

As they waited for the Lord's perfect timing, the price of homes in their area decreased in value over the next two years. In the end, they paid a significantly lower price and assumed a smaller mortgage than expected. The Lord had blessed them for waiting. They praised the Lord!

I recommend you reflect on each question and write your own answers before reviewing my comments.

QUESTION #1
What biblical financial principles did Ralph and Deborah follow? Please provide a Scripture reference for each point.

TOM'S COMMENT

Here are the biblical financial principles that Ralph and Deborah wisely followed.

- First and foremost, they prayed and asked God for his wisdom (James 1:5) and his specific direction (Psalm 32:8).
- Seeking the Lord's counsel is essential and always helpful. Jehoshaphat said to the King of Israel in 1 Kings 22:5: "First seek the counsel of the LORD."
- They paid off their current debts before taking on additional debt, such as a mortgage. Romans 13:8 states, "Let no debt remain outstanding."
- They developed a "future budget" or a "cash flow projection" to determine what they could afford. According to Proverbs 21:5, "The plans of the diligent lead to profit as surely as haste leads to poverty."
- As they saved for a house, they spent quality time in prayer with the Lord and recorded in their journals what they discerned God wanted them to do. As a couple, it was appropriate that they compared what they sensed to be the Lord's direction. God desires husbands and wives to agree on significant decisions before proceeding. Genesis 2:24 defines a husband and wife as "one flesh."
- Ralph and Deborah *chose to be content* with a smaller home, even though they could have borrowed more money and bought a larger home. They followed the apostle Paul's teaching in 1 Timothy 6:6–8, which says: "Godliness with contentment is great gain. For we have brought nothing into this world, and we will take nothing out of it. But if we have food and clothing, we will be content with that."
- They received biblical financial guidance from a godly financial adviser who had no personal interest in selling them

anything and who was independent of the real estate agents (Proverbs 15:22; Psalm 1:1–3).

Ralph and Deborah waited about seven years for God to provide them with a house that they could afford comfortably. In Isaiah 64:4, we are told that God "acts on behalf of those who wait for him."

Most importantly, they studied God's word on finances and diligently applied His biblical principles to manage the money the Lord entrusted to them. Second Timothy 3:16–17 tells us: "All Scripture is God-breathed and is useful for teaching, rebuking, correcting and training in righteousness, so that the servant of God may be thoroughly equipped for every good work."

QUESTION #2
What were Ralph and Deborah's three sources of biblical counsel?

TOM'S COMMENT
Ralph and Deborah were wise to utilize the following three sources of advice.

1. God Himself was their first and most important source of counsel. Isaiah 28:29 states, "All this comes from the LORD Almighty, whose plan is wonderful, whose wisdom is magnificent." Ralph and Deborah spent considerable time in prayer over two years, asking God for guidance according to His will (Psalm 32:8).
2. Ralph and Deborah studied what the Bible says about finances, which applies to the critical decision to purchase

a home. Psalm 119:24 states, "Your statutes are my delight; they are my counselors."

3. Finally, they sought the advice of a godly financial adviser. Proverbs 12:15 states, "The way of fools seems right to them, but the wise listen to advice."

QUESTION #3

What do you think is different about Ralph and Deborah's approach to this important financial decision compared to what others may do? Support your answer with a Scripture reference.

TOM'S COMMENT

Unlike most people, Ralph and Deborah took a very different approach when making this major decision to purchase their home. For example:

- They obeyed God despite their own desires (Acts 5:29).
- They waited upon the Lord for His perfect timing (Psalm 37:7).
- In faith, they *trusted God's counsel* not to purchase a house when they wanted to (Proverbs 3:5–6; Acts 27:25).
- They spent quality time in prayer and asked God for His wisdom (see James 1:5), and listened to God's voice (John 10:27) to discern God's specific plan for their lives (Jeremiah 29:11–13).

QUESTION #4

Ralph and Deborah spent considerable time in prayer listening for God's voice (John 10:27) and asking the Lord to give them

His peace or lack of peace regarding buying a house. *Did God bless this approach*?

TOM'S COMMENT

Absolutely! As they prayed and waited patiently on Him, God blessed them and provided a lovely semi-detached home that was within their means and did not cause *financial stress* after the purchase, which is so common.

QUESTION #5

Is this approach common? Please write your thoughts below.

TOM'S COMMENT

Unfortunately, no. Even Christians seldom follow a biblical approach to managing their finances or when making major financial decisions.

QUESTION #6

Did Ralph and Deborah take a biblical approach to their finances? Please explain with a reference to Scripture.

TOM'S COMMENT

Yes, absolutely! According to Jeremiah 29:11–13, God has a specific plan for each of his children, and God promises to direct each of us (Psalm 32:8). However, God wants to bless us according to His will, not ours. David wrote in Psalm 40:8, "I desire to do your will, my God; your law is within my heart."

Every Christian should desire to do God's will, to do what He wants them to do, even if it's not what they want. The specific plan and will of God are far more beneficial to us in the long run than our own.

Further, Ralph and Deborah waited until they experienced God's peace before making a final financial decision. In John 14: 27, Jesus said, "Peace I leave with you; my peace I give you. I do not give to you as the world gives. Do not let your hearts be troubled and do not be afraid."

QUESTION #7

In Psalm 32:8, God tells his followers, "I will instruct you and teach you in the way you should go; I will counsel you with my loving eye on you." In what ways does God instruct and counsel us? Please provide a Scripture reference for each point.

TOM'S COMMENT

The following are some ways God instructs us.

- In response to prayer, God can provide peace or lack of peace concerning a contemplated course of action (John 14:26–27).
- God can instruct and counsel us through His word (Psalm 119:105). As you prayerfully review God's word, the Holy

Spirit can direct you by highlighting specific passages that address your situation (John 14:15–17, 26).

- During our quiet times, God can speak to our hearts and minds via a "gentle whisper" (1 Kings 19:12; John 10:3–4).
- God can direct us through godly counsel (Proverbs 15:22; Psalm 1:1–3).
- Jesus promised in John 10:27, "My sheep listen to My voice, and I know them, and they follow Me" (NASB).
- God can open and close doors according to His will (Psalm 103:19).

QUESTION #8

In your opinion, are circumstances important? How critical are they in making a significant financial decision?

TOM'S COMMENT

Circumstances are important, but we must consider them alongside the following.

- All decisions must align with God's financial principles as outlined in the Bible (2 Timothy 3:16–17).
- I believe that asking God in prayer for His specific direction (Psalm 119:35) and waiting on the Lord for His instruction (Psalm 37:7) are more important than our circumstances.
- God directed Gideon through his circumstances by a fleece (Judges 6:36–40). However, this resulted from his personal relationship with God. God had already spoken to Gideon about what he should do (Judges 6:12–14), and the fleece was merely a confirmation, not a direct revelation.

Above all, *our relationship with Christ is paramount.* Jesus used the analogy of a shepherd and his sheep to explain that when we develop a close relationship with God, we can hear His voice and follow His lead. John 10:3–4 reads: "The gate-keeper opens the gate for him, and the sheep listen to his voice. He calls his own sheep by name and leads them out. When he has brought out all his own, he goes on ahead of them, and his sheep follow him because they know his voice."

QUESTION #9

A real estate expert advised Ralph and Deborah to buy their home as soon as possible because they were confident that the value of real estate would continue to increase.

Consider Proverbs 27:1, "Do not boast about tomorrow, for you do not know what a day may bring." What is the core meaning of God's warning?

TOM'S COMMENT

Human beings are incapable of predicting the future. Therefore, it is essential to spend quality time with the Lord before making any significant financial decision, seeking His specific guidance.

Unfortunately, believers often make decisions without consulting God, and later suffer the consequences. In the absence of God's clear direction, we inevitably choose God's second-best and simply make terrible choices.

QUESTION #10

According to Proverbs 27:1 and James 4:13–15, people cannot predict the future. Knowing the future and controlling what happens in this life would be a tremendous asset in making financial decisions!

Does anyone know the future? Is anyone in control of what is going on in our society? Who is it? Consider these Scriptures; then write your comments:

Psalm 103:19 states, "The Lord has established his throne in heaven, and his kingdom rules over all."

Isaiah 46:9–11 states: "I am God, and there is no other; I am God, and there is none like me. *I make known the end from the beginning*, from ancient times, *what is still to come*. I say, '*My purpose will stand, and I will do all that I please … What I have said, that I will bring about; what I have planned, that I will do*" (emphasis added).

TOM'S COMMENT

Only God knows the future (2 Kings 7:1–19; Isaiah 46:10), and only God is in control (Psalm 103:19). Remember in Genesis 41, God revealed the future to Pharaoh in a dream—seven years of prosperity and seven years of famine. Then God explicitly revealed the meaning of the dream to Joseph. In short, God knew the future then, and He knows the future today.

QUESTION #11

Given that only God knows the future, what implications does that have for your life, especially when making major financial decisions?

TOM'S COMMENT

When making financial decisions, it is vital to seek God's wisdom and direction (James 1:5) and not rely on your own limited knowledge and understanding, or even that of others (Proverbs 3:5–6).

QUESTION #12

To conclude, if you truly desire to make an informed financial decision that is consistent with God's will, what do you need to do?

TOM'S COMMENT

It is important to spend quality time with the Lord in prayer (Psalm 5:3).

Keep an attentive ear to hear His voice (John 10:27), read His word (2 Timothy 3:16), seek godly counsel as He directs (Proverbs 12:15), and wait upon God (Psalm 37:7) for His specific direction (Psalm 32:8) for your life.

As God provides his specific instructions, it is critical to obey him (Deuteronomy 28:1–12) and trust Him for the results (Proverbs 3:5–6).

Discuss the relevance and application of the following verses with regard to Ralph and Deborah's situation. Write your comments below each verse.

"Your word is a lamp for my feet, a light on my path" (Psalm 119:105).

TOM'S COMMENT

Ralph and Deborah studied God's word before purchasing a home. God's word provided "a light" regarding God's financial principles, which the worldly experts had not provided. And God used His word to direct them when and which house they should buy.

"My sheep listen to my voice; I know them, and they follow me" (John 10:27).

TOM'S COMMENT

During their prayer time, Ralph and Deborah listened to God's voice and followed His guidance, and they were blessed accordingly.

Now listen, you who say, "Today or tomorrow we will go to this or that city, spend a year there, carry on business and make money." Why, you do not even know what will happen tomorrow. What is your life? You are a mist that appears for a little while and then vanishes. Instead, you ought to say, "If it is the Lord's will, we will live and do this or that." (James 4:13–15)

TOM'S COMMENT

Ralph and Deborah learned from God's word and acknowledged that no human being can predict the future. In response, they decided not to rely on the advice of worldly realtors who believed that housing prices would never decrease. Instead, Ralph and Deborah sought God's guidance and wisdom for the important financial decision to buy a house.

Read the following passage in 2 Kings 7:1–16 and consider the key biblical principles.

In 2 Kings 7:1, 6–7, 16, the price of food initially skyrocketed (they had hyperinflation) because of a severe shortage of food. Everyone in the city believed they would die of hunger, except for Elijah, the prophet. He predicted God would do something *extraordinary* and provide a surplus of food, causing food prices to return to normal. And indeed, God performed a miracle, fulfilling the prophecy that God gave Elisha.

> Elisha replied, "Hear the word of the LORD. This is what the LORD says: About this time tomorrow, a seah of the finest flour will sell for a shekel and two seahs of barley for a shekel at the gate of Samaria." ... The Lord had caused the Arameans to hear the sound of chariots and horses and a great army, so that they said to one another, "Look, the king of Israel has hired the Hittite and Egyptian kings to attack us!" So they got up and fled in the dusk

and abandoned their tents and their horses and donkeys. They left the camp as it was and ran for their lives … Then the people went out and plundered the camp of the Arameans. So a seah of the finest flour sold for a shekel, and two seahs of barley sold for a shekel, as the LORD had said. (2 Kings 7:1, 6–7, 16)

TOM'S COMMENT

The key principle in the above passage is that only God knows the future. Accordingly, Ralph and Deborah depended solely on God to provide instructions regarding what to do and when to do it. As a result, they were blessed by waiting to buy a house. Praise God!

"Everything in the heavens and earth is yours, O Lord, and this is your kingdom. We adore you as being in control of everything. Riches and honor come from you alone, and you are the ruler of all mankind; your hand controls power and might, and it is at your discretion that men are made great and given strength" (1 Chronicles 29:11–12 TLB).

TOM'S COMMENT

Ralph and Deborah had faith that God was in control and could provide them with the right house, at the right time, and at the right price, as ordained by the Lord.

"The Lord has established His throne in the heavens, and His sovereignty rules over all" (Psalm 103:19, NASB).

TOM'S COMMENT

The absolute truth is that God is ultimately in control of everything that happens on this earth. Even though God allows things to happen that we cannot understand, He is always in control. Ralph and Deborah understood this biblical truth and trusted God to meet their needs as they put Him first in their financial planning (see Matthew 6:31–33).

10. Case Study #2: A Couple "Steps Out in Faith"

Henry and Melinda are married. They have worked full-time for three years and earn average incomes. They plan to start a family soon and anticipate needing a good-sized home. However, they have no savings and incurred substantial debt while attending university. Additionally, they have not tracked their expenses or developed and implemented a budget. Yet they pray about a newly listed house on the market and firmly believe that God wants them to purchase the house.

They approach their parents, who agree to provide them with a down payment. The bank also approves them for a substantial mortgage since they both have stable, full-time employment. Furthermore, a Christian realtor selling the house encourages them to borrow as much as necessary and trust God for the loan payments. As a result, they sense God wants them to "step out in faith" and buy the house at the maximum price they can borrow. Henry and Melinda purchase the house.

After a couple of years, it becomes evident that they are in financial trouble. Aside from their school loans, they have run up significant credit card debt. In response, they resort to "debt restructuring" by obtaining a line of credit from their bank to pay off their credit cards. Over the next couple of years, their credit card balances and line of credit reach their maximum. Consequently, they cannot meet their financial obligations, and the bank and credit card companies will not lend them any more money.

They explain the situation to their parents, who agree to loan them enough to pay off their credit cards. Henry and Melinda believe they have solved their financial problems. However, they did not alter their money management habits. Rather, they continue to spend more than they earn. After another year, they have maxed out their credit sources again!

They approach their parents for another loan, but their parents refuse to lend them any more money. Henry and Melinda are under a great deal of financial stress, which causes them to argue daily. As a result of severe financial pressures, they are now in danger of separating or divorcing for the first time in their relationship.

At about the same time, Melinda discovers she is pregnant. They have always dreamed of having a family, and Melinda wants to stay home with their new baby. However, because of their dire financial situation, this is no longer an option since she will have to work full-time to help service their debt.

QUESTION #1

What biblical financial principles did Henry and Melinda violate? Please write your answers to each question, and provide a Scripture reference before reading my comments.

TOM'S COMMENT

Henry and Melinda violated the following biblical financial principles.

- They did not pray and ask God for His wisdom (James 1:5) or His specific direction (Psalm 25:12) before purchasing the house.
- They did not consider what God's word on finances said before making this major financial decision. As a result, they did not take a biblical approach to purchasing their house (Psalm 119:105).
- They did not develop and implement a budget to ensure they had sufficient cash flow to cover their mortgage and other house-related expenses, such as property taxes, utilities, maintenance, and insurance—as well as paying down the previous debts they accumulated! They had no cash flow plan. In Luke 14:28–30, Jesus instructed that planning and preparing a budget beforehand is a practical and biblical way to manage your finances.
- They did not track their expenses, so they did not know where their money was going (Proverbs 27:23). In other words, they did not know their *financial facts.* As the saying goes, they were "flying by the seat of their pants."
- They bought a house based on personal desire rather than need. In Matthew 6:31–33, Christ promised to meet our needs as we put Him first, but He did not promise to meet our personal wants and desires.
- They did not seek independent biblically based financial advice. Unfortunately, the realtor's advice was inconsistent with God's word (Psalm 1:1–3; Proverbs 15:22).
- They were in the habit of spending all of their income and more. This was demonstrated by the fact that they had accumulated significant debt while students. Although they

had worked full-time for several years before purchasing a house, they had not paid off their previous debt or saved a reasonable down payment. Instead, they continued to spend all their regular income. Proverbs 21:20 states, "A wise man saves for the future, but the foolish man spends whatever he gets" (TLB).

QUESTION #2

Henry and Melinda indicated they had prayed. They sincerely believed that God directed them to purchase the house, borrow the down payment, and take on a sizable mortgage. Based on God's word, do you think God was directing them?

TOM'S COMMENT

They may have prayed, but I'm confident they did not hear clearly from the Lord. The reason is that in the process of purchasing the house, they violated at least seven biblical financial principles as outlined above.

Never forget that God would never lead His children to do anything that is contrary to His word. It is more likely that Henry and Melinda went ahead with the purchase of their house because of their own personal desires.

QUESTION #3

Henry and Melinda claimed they "stepped out in faith" when they purchased their home and assumed a lot of debt. What prerequisites should be met before a committed Christian truly "steps out in faith" and borrows a significant amount of money? Please provide a Scripture reference for each point.

TOM'S COMMENT

A Christian should step out in faith only after doing the following.

- In prayer, sincerely ask God for His wisdom (James 1:5) and His specific direction (Psalm 25:12) as to what He wants you to do.
- Pray to the Lord as Jesus did in Luke 22:42: "Yet not my will, but yours be done." In other words, be willing to do God's will *even if it's less than what you want.* It is essential to base your financial decisions on your financial facts rather than feelings or emotions.
- Study what God's word (Psalm 119:105) says regarding such a financial decision, including debt (Deuteronomy 28:1–44), God's promise to meet our needs (Philippians 4:19), and the risks of borrowing money (Proverbs 22:7).
- Prepare a budget to determine whether you can afford your desired purchase. Proverbs 21:5 reminds us, "The plans of the diligent lead to profit as surely as haste leads to poverty." Henry and Melinda made impulsive decisions, which

led to major financial problems that were so serious that it threatened their relationship.

- Before proceeding with a significant purchase, like a house, review your expenses over the last year or two to determine where your money has gone. If you've earned a good income, as in Henry and Melinda's case, you should have paid off any school loans and saved some money towards a down payment. Unfortunately, Henry and Melinda failed to do this. Since both had decent incomes, they likely spent too much on "wants and desires" instead of needs. They must learn to be content with less (Luke 3:14).
- Be sure that you, and your spouse if you are married, seek the advice of a godly financial adviser (1 Corinthians 2:14–15).
- Proceed only after you have spent sufficient time with the Lord in prayer, waiting upon God (Psalm 37:7), and after receiving God's peace about the decision (John 14:26–27).

TOM'S GENERAL COMMENTS ON CASE STUDY #2 AND "STEPPING OUT IN FAITH"

Henry and Melinda's circumstances and their approach to financial decision-making are all too common around the world. First, I would like to ask: Why didn't Henry and Melinda pay off their student loans and save a reasonable amount for a down payment on a house after working full-time for several years and earning average incomes? The answer is that although they both worked full-time, they spent more than they earned and lived paycheque-to-paycheque. According to Proverbs 21:20 and Luke 14:28–30, this is foolish. Individuals who mismanage their finances in such a way will eventually suffer the consequences.

Further, Christ warned that if someone is not trustworthy with a small amount, they will not be trustworthy with a large amount (Luke 16:10). Therefore, it is risky for a couple with poor money management skills to take on a large mortgage.

Of interest, I have seen hundreds of cases where parents have loaned money to their children for a down payment on a home. If the children have a history of being poor money managers, there is a high probability that their bad habits will continue, and they will never repay their parents. This will likely cause tension between the adult children and their parents and conflict between siblings who did not receive the same benefits.

For these reasons, I highly recommend that parents do not give or lend a significant amount of money to their children until they show they can manage money wisely, according to biblical principles. You could otherwise enable them to continue in their destructive financial habits, allowing them to take on debt they will probably never repay. This is a serious matter, considering Psalm 37:21, which says that "the wicked borrow and do not repay."

11. Case Study #3: A Single Woman Obtains Financial Advice

Brenda is a single woman who earns an average income. She has worked hard during the past couple of years, followed a budget, spent wisely, and borrowed minimally. She praises the Lord because she just paid off her loans—no mortgage, no car loan, and no credit card balances—no debt whatsoever! She sleeps much better at night, knowing that she has no liabilities.

When her financial adviser, Karl, heard that Brenda was debt-free, he suggested she borrow against her home and invest it in mutual funds to get the equity in her home working for her. He explained that the interest would be deductible and that many of his clients had done this and benefited from significant returns. He told her, "Smart people use other people's money."

Brenda wasn't sure what to do, but she remembered from our in-depth biblical financial study "Financial Management God's Way" that God's word recommends seeking biblical financial advice from God (1 Kings 22:5), God's word (Psalm 119:105), and a godly financial adviser (Psalm 1:1–3).

She searched God's word and learned that God discouraged debt (Proverbs 22:7) and that God promised His people that if they obeyed Him fully, He would bless them to be lenders and not borrowers (Deuteronomy 28:1–12). Additionally, she sought biblically based financial advice from a second adviser named Eli. He advised her not to borrow. Rather, he encouraged her to develop a budget to have a surplus each month to invest in a diversified portfolio, according to Ecclesiastes 11:2. Eli explained that if she invested a little every month over a long period, following biblical principles, she would receive some reasonable returns. Eli quoted Proverbs 13:11, "Whoever gathers money little by little makes it grow." And Proverbs 21:5 states, "Steady plodding brings prosperity; hasty speculation brings poverty" (TLB).

Brenda opted to follow Eli's advice over Karl's, her current financial adviser. She soon let Karl go and hired Eli, who provided her with sound biblical guidance.

Here's my definition of a godly financial adviser:

1. Is a spiritually mature Christian.
2. Understands and applies God's financial principles (Psalm 111:10).
3. Has a close personal relationship with the Lord (John 15).
4. Has the necessary practical financial knowledge (Proverbs 24:3–4).

5. Habitually puts the interests of clients first (Philippians 2:3–4).

QUESTION #1

Consider these five characteristics, and identify which ones Karl and Eli met. Please write your answers below before reading my comments.

TOM'S COMMENT

Eli displayed all five characteristics of a godly financial adviser when he counseled Brenda. Karl, on the other hand, gave advice that was not consistent with God's word. One could conclude that Karl is not a spiritually mature Christian, as he did not understand basic biblical financial principles related to investing, which should be his area of expertise.

Additionally, Karl likely does not have a close relationship with God, as he put his interests before Brenda's. Finally, Karl had some practical knowledge of finance, but he provided worldly advice mainly for his benefit. Clearly, Karl does not qualify as a godly financial adviser.

QUESTION #2

Assessing whether a financial adviser meets the requirements of "a godly financial adviser" may be difficult. In light of this standard, how would you evaluate a prospective financial adviser? Write your answer below.

TOM'S COMMENT

- Ask prospective financial advisers to explain their preferred approach and strategy to financial planning and investing, using real-life examples (Proverbs 24:3–4).
- Obtain information about the adviser's track record over the past few years. Ask for the names and phone numbers of present clients, and check those references.
- Ask whether the adviser recommends the use of debt (Proverbs 22:7).
- Assess the adviser's knowledge of God's financial principles by asking specific questions related to biblical knowledge.
- Confirm from an independent source(s) the adviser's character and credentials.
- If practical, try to network and get some references of people who have used their services for whom they *did not provide* a reference. Financial advisers are not going to provide references for clients who had a negative experience with them previously.
- Throughout the process, pray and ask God to lead you.

QUESTION #3

In the long run, whose clients are likely to do better on their investments, Karl's or Eli's?

TOM'S COMMENT

Eli's clients will likely fare better in the long run, with far less volatility than Karl's clients. Additionally, Eli's clients may benefit from "dollar-cost averaging" by investing a fixed amount each month over a long period, which is especially important when investing in equities. Karl's clients will assume significantly more risk and volatility than Eli's clients by borrowing to invest.

QUESTION #4
Who do you think would earn the most commissions initially, with respect to the two strategies proposed by Karl and Eli?

TOM'S COMMENT
The lump-sum investment Karl wanted Brenda to make with the money she borrowed from the bank would initially earn Karl a much higher commission than Eli.

QUESTION #5
What does this likely reflect about Karl's and Eli's character?

TOM'S COMMENT
Karl may have been motivated by greed and selfishness (Luke 12:15). On the other hand, Eli prioritized the interests of his clients (Philippians 2:3–4). Eli's biblically based financial planning and investing advice satisfy both his godly character and his biblical approach. Therefore, Eli and his clients are likely to surpass Karl and his clients in terms of long-term financial success—and with fewer sleepless nights because of the lessened risk.

Of interest, over the past four decades, I have seen many cases where people have borrowed money to increase investment returns. Unfortunately, the results were often disastrous, or their portfolio's volatility was so significant that the individuals lost a lot of sleep. In my experience, people who invested a fixed amount of their own money each month over a long period ended up much better off financially than those who used debt to increase returns. It should come as no surprise that this latter approach has more success since it is consistent with the financial principles outlined in God's word.

In summary, God's word discourages debt (Proverbs 22:7; Deuteronomy 28:1–2, 12, 15, 43–44) and encourages saving and investing a little at a time over an extended period, like the monthly contributions that Eli suggested (Proverbs 13:11). In other words, use the strategy of dollar-cost averaging, particularly with investing in equities,

12. Co-Signing

Co-signing is a debt-related topic. Most people are unaware that God's word strongly advises against co-signing. The terminology used for co-signing in the New International Version of the book of Proverbs is to "strike hands in pledge."

When Proverbs was written, they did not have lengthy legal documents for their agreements; a handshake was sufficient. "To strike hands in pledge" meant to shake hands confirming your pledge to pay a financial obligation. God warns that if you "strike hands in pledge" or co-sign for a debt, something very negative could happen to you. According to Proverbs 22:26–27: "Do not be one who shakes hands in pledge or puts up security for debts; if you lack the means to pay, your very bed will be snatched from under you."

A contemporary analogy to having your bed "snatched out from under you" is losing something valuable, such as your home or retirement fund.

God's word concerning co-signing is a principle, not a law. It is not a sin to co-sign, but God warns that if you co-sign, you may suffer some negative consequences. Proverbs 17:18 is very clear regarding the risks associated with co-signing: "A man lacking common sense gives a pledge and becomes guarantor [for the debt of another] in the presence of his neighbor" (AMP).

The concept of co-signing is easier to understand in the Contemporary English Version (CEV), which provides the following Proverbs.

Proverbs 11:15 says, "It's a dangerous thing to guarantee payment for someone's debts. Don't do it!"

Proverbs 22:26–27 says, "Don't guarantee to pay someone else's debt. If you don't have the money, you might lose your bed."

In conclusion, the Bible clearly discourages Christians from guaranteeing someone else's debt. As a result of decades of experience, I have found that about 70 per cent of the time, when someone co-signs a loan for another, even if it is a relative, the co-signer is forced to pay the debt, not the borrower. This is not surprising since the bank insists on a co-signer in the first place because it doesn't trust the borrower is creditworthy.

13. Case Study #4: A Couple Co-Signs on Their Son's Loan

Bill and Jenny co-signed a loan for their son and daughter-in-law without realizing the implications. After several years, the son and his wife ran into financial difficulties and missed several loan payments. Finally, the bank lost patience and legally demanded the loan, then unilaterally paid it off using the co-signers' money.

Bill and Jenny were stunned as they read the legal document that explained the bank had seized a significant portion of their retirement fund. Aside from losing a lot of money, Bill and Jenny lost their excellent relationship with their son and daughter-in-law, who felt guilty. Invitations to dinner were declined, and both parties found getting together awkward at best. It was regrettable that co-signing had strained their relationship and gone so wrong.

Answer the following questions, and give it your best effort to write down your suggested solutions before reading my comments. Give a reference to Scripture for each point you make.

QUESTION #1
Did Bill and Jenny violate any biblical principles when they co-signed?

TOM'S COMMENT
Yes, Bill and Jenny did not heed God's word that clearly warns of the dangers of co-signing (Proverbs 11:15; 17:8; 22:25–26).

QUESTION #2
If someone were to ask you to co-sign a loan for them, how would you respond?

TOM'S COMMENT

I highly recommend people adopt a policy to never co-sign a loan for anyone because *co-signing is contrary to God's financial principles*. However, if there is a genuine need, and if led by the Lord, give or lend money and expect nothing in return (Luke 6:32–38). In this way, your relationship with each other should remain intact.

QUESTION #3

What should you do if you've already co-signed on a loan? For an answer, read Proverbs 6:1–5:

> My son, if you have put up security for your neighbor, if you have shaken hands in pledge for a stranger, you have been trapped by what you said, ensnared by the words of your mouth. So do this, my son, to free yourself, since you have fallen into your neighbor's hands: Go—to the point of exhaustion—and give your neighbor no rest! Allow no sleep to your eyes, no slumber to your eyelids. Free yourself, like a gazelle from the hand of the hunter, like a bird from the snare of the fowler.

A more modern version, The Passion Translation, puts it this way:

> My son, if you co-sign a loan for an acquaintance and guarantee his debt, you'll be sorry that you ever did it! You'll be trapped by your promise and legally bound by the agreement. So listen carefully to my advice: Quickly get out of it if you possibly can! Swallow your pride, get over your embarrassment, and go tell your "friend" you want your name off that contract. Don't put it off, and don't rest until you get it done. Rescue yourself from future pain

and be free from it once and for all. You'll be so relieved that you did!

TOM'S COMMENT

As shown in the above passages, co-signing for someone else's loan is a serious matter. God's counsel is to "free yourself" as soon as possible from the co-signed loan! Better yet, it is best to never enter into a co-signing agreement in the first place.

QUESTION #4

What are some practical ways to free yourself from the financial obligations of a co-signed loan?

TOM'S COMMENT

- Pray and ask God for His wisdom (James 1:5). Some situations may require a *miracle* from God in order to free you from the obligation.
- Try to find another bank that would lend the borrower money without a co-signer. Then use these funds to pay off the loan you had to pay.
- Encourage and help the borrower to learn how to manage their finances according to biblical principles, which would reduce the risk of default.

QUESTION #5

If a friend or relative has a need and asks you to co-sign a loan, what are some other options to help them *without* co-signing?

TOM'S COMMENT

- Pray about the situation, and if you sense God's leading, and they are good money managers, give or lend them the money they need.
- If God directs you to lend money, do so, but be prepared to forgive the loan if necessary (Luke 6:35). In this way, the relationship will remain intact even if the loan is never repaid.
- Provide biblically based financial counsel, or refer them to a godly financial adviser. Although a person may request a loan, often what they really need is to learn how to manage money according to God's principles.

QUESTION #6

If adult children get into financial difficulty, should the parents "bail them out"? Please write your thoughts before reading my comments.

TOM'S COMMENT

God may direct you to lend to your adult children in certain situations, but make sure you prayerfully consider this before you do. As a general rule, parents should not bail out their grown children who have mismanaged money, because if you do, you enable them to continue with their poor money management habits. Nothing will be resolved.

Adults need to understand and apply God's financial principles rather than have someone else pay off their debts. Furthermore, Christians often grow spiritually the most during difficult times, and you should not interfere with that spiritual growth.

In the end, they need to learn that God is their ultimate source of provision for all things, including financial resources. This lesson may come through the trial of financial hardship.

QUESTION #7

Discuss the relevance and application of the following Scriptural verses with regard to Bill and Jenny's situation. Write your comments for each verse.

"Do not be one who shakes hands in pledge or puts up security for debts; if you lack the means to pay, your very bed will be snatched from under you" (Proverbs 22:26–27).

TOM'S COMMENT

Unfortunately, Bill and Jenny did not follow God's wisdom to not co-sign. Consequently, they lost a part of their retirement fund and their relationship with their son and daughter-in-law.

"Whoever puts up security for a stranger will surely suffer, but whoever refuses to shake hands in pledge is safe" (Proverbs 11:15).

TOM'S COMMENT

By co-signing, Bill and Jenny put up security (in this case, their retirement fund) for their son and his wife. As a result, they suffered significant losses. Unfortunately, they did not heed God's wisdom and directive, which is to refuse to co-sign—do not "strike hands in pledge."

14. A Single Father Co-Signs a Son's Automobile Loan

During one of my interviews on a live radio show, a father called in to share that he had co-signed on an automobile loan for his adult son. The father was confident that his son earned enough money to pay for his car loan and other expenses comfortably. He was unaware, however, that his son was a terrible money manager.

Consequently, the son missed several loan payments, which resulted in the bank sending a threatening letter to the father demanding full payment for the overdue loan installments. As you can imagine, the father was quite upset, which caused tension between him and his son.

To worsen matters, this negatively impacted the father's credit rating to the extent that his financial institution refused to renew his mortgage when it came due months later. As a result, the father had no option but to obtain private mortgage financing at a much higher interest rate.

His father argued with the bank, explaining that the loan wasn't his but rather his son's, and his son was the one who defaulted. Nevertheless, the bank treated the father as one of the borrowers because he had co-signed the loan. As a result, the *father's credit rating was negatively affected when his son missed loan payments.*

Generally speaking, if you co-sign a loan and the borrower defaults, you will not only have a bad credit score, but you may face the following:

- Your poor credit rating may prevent you from renting a place.
- You may have difficulty qualifying for a loan to buy something you need, like a car.
- Your poor credit rating could cost you an employment opportunity. Employers are increasingly checking credit reports as part of the hiring process, especially for management positions.

15. A Single Mother Co-Signs a Friend's Business Loan

On another occasion, I was interviewed on a live call-in program with another radio station. This is a sad story. After years of hard work and careful financial management, a single mother of two finally paid off her mortgage. She was entirely debt-free.

Her close friend wanted to start a business, but she had no start-up capital. However, the bank was willing to lend her friend a large sum of money if she could find a co-signer for a business loan. The single mother co-signed the loan for her friend, believing there would be no foreseeable problems. Also, she trusted her friend implicitly, as they had been friends for decades and had a close relationship.

Unfortunately, her friend's business got into financial trouble and eventually went bankrupt. The friend could not pay her loan, so the bank took legal action against the co-signer. This single mother lost her home. She was in tears when she told me her story, and my heart went out to her. Sadly, this Christian woman could have avoided this unfortunate situation had she understood God's directive in His word *not to co-sign* on any loans!

16. Co-Signing Reduces Borrowing Capacity

Here's another typical example. You co-sign a loan for someone, and they manage their money well and make their payments on time. Everything appears to be fine with no repercussions for you as a co-signer. However, this is not necessarily true.

Consider this scenario. Your dream home just came on the market, and you want to put in an offer. You go to the bank to apply for a "pre-approved mortgage" only to discover you don't qualify to borrow nearly as much as you expected and need. When you find out the bank included the debt you co-signed on in their calculations, you are shocked. As a result, your debt-to-income ratio is too high, even though the debt for which you co-signed is not actually yours—but from the bank's perspective, it is your debt as well.

Consequently, your mortgage application is denied, and you cannot purchase your dream home. It seems unfair, especially since the person you co-signed for is responsible and pays their bills on time.

Unfortunately, most banks operate this way and include the debt as yours, since you are essentially responsible for it. The same principle applies no matter what you want to finance—a condo, automobile, or business start-up.

17. Recommended Steps to Take Before Co-Signing

God's directive not to co-sign is a principle, not a law. In some cases, there can be considerable pressure on an individual to co-sign for another's loan. The person could be a close family member, such as a son or daughter, a sibling, a parent, or a close friend. Each could have a genuine need and require a co-signer to buy what they need.

Before you seriously consider co-signing for someone, what steps should you take, and what questions should you ask before agreeing to co-sign?

I came up with ten suggested steps to consider. Please list as many as you can, and provide a reference to Scripture before reading my comments.

TOM'S COMMENT

- Find out the borrower's money management history. In Luke 16:10 (CSB), Jesus said, "Whoever is faithful in very little is also faithful in much, and whoever is unrighteous in very little is also unrighteous in much." This is a critical point because people who have not been faithful in managing their money so far are unlikely to be faithful in managing even more money. This increases the risk of default, placing the co-signer at risk of having to pay back the loan.

• A question to ask is whether the potential borrower spends money on necessities or is frivolous. In other words, do they spend too much on wants and desires? According to Matthew 6:31–33, God promises to meet our needs but not necessarily our wants and desires.

• Are they content to live within the income that God has provided (1 Timothy 6:6–8)? If the answer is no, then it's best not to co-sign.

• Has the borrower developed a plan (Proverbs 21:5), that is, a budget to ensure they can afford the loan payments? On that note, I recommend you *review their budget and make sure it's realistic before you co-sign for them.*

• Concerning the specific purchase they want you to co-sign for, determine if it is a genuine need or want or desire (Philippians 4:19). If it's the latter, then generally do not co-sign.

• Does this individual or couple understand their responsibility to repay the entire loan (Psalm 37:21) and make the payments on time (Matthew 5:16) even if you were to co-sign? Be careful to make certain that the borrower knows it is their responsibility to pay their loan, not the co-signer's! I have seen cases where the borrower thinks the co-signer is responsible for paying the loan, not the borrower.

• Has the borrower prayerfully reviewed the list in "Questions to Consider before Borrowing" before coming to you and asking you to co-sign? Make sure that they've done everything they can do to avoid the debt in the first place.

• Most importantly, have you, as the potential co-signer, spent sufficient time with the Lord in prayer seeking God's will to discern if He wants you to co-sign on the loan (Luke 22:42)?

- Further, do not assume that the borrower will pay off their loan and everything will be fine (James 4:11–13). Basically, *if you cannot afford to pay the loan should the borrower default, you should not co-sign on the loan!*
- It is at *the planning stage that God will frequently direct us* if we take time to discern His will. Proverbs 16:3 says, "Commit your actions to the Lord, and your plans will succeed" (NLT).

C. A SUMMARY OF WHAT THE BIBLE SAYS ON DEBT AND CO-SIGNING: BIBLICAL PERSPECTIVE VERSUS WORLDLY PERSPECTIVE

The biblical perspective is to use minimal debt or ideally no debt. The worldly perspective is to use debt freely which results in lots of debt. God warns of the dangers of cosigning; avoid it whenever you can. The world, especially the banking industry, encourages cosigning.

To learn more about both the borrower and co-signer, please visit our website at www.coplandfinancialministries.org and watch the eight thirty-minute videos titled "Discerning God's Will."

18. Personal Guarantees for Corporate Debt Are a Form of Co-Signing

Christian business owners often fail to recognize that when they take out personal guarantees regarding their company's debt, they are technically co-signing a loan, which God discourages. The same Scriptures outlined above apply to business owners. For example, Proverbs 22:26–27 says, "Don't guarantee to pay someone else's debt. If you don't have the money, you might lose your bed" (CEV).

Since 1982, I have managed my own public accounting firm, focusing on private owner-managed corporations. I encourage and help these business owners to reduce their corporate and personal debt and to avoid giving a personal guarantee for their corporation's debt.

Of course, the best level of debt to have is *nothing*. However, as a practical matter, I understand that business owners often need loans to finance equipment, vehicles, inventory, and accounts receivable.

Let's suppose your company must take on some corporate debt. In that case, I highly recommend you assume as little debt as possible and do everything you can to avoid giving your personal guarantee, so that your personal assets, such as your home and your retirement fund, are not at risk.

Assuming you have already provided your personal guarantee to the bank, here are some suggestions to "free yourself" from corporate guarantees (Proverbs 6:1–5).

- As usual, pray and ask God for His wisdom (James 1:5) and His specific direction (Psalm 32:8) as to how you can be released from the corporate guarantee. Often, a miracle is required because once banks have your personal guarantee, they generally don't want to lose it.
- Before going to another bank, at least attempt to negotiate with your current bank to release your personal guarantee. If the answer is no, then consider the following suggestions.
- Network through business associates, and find a bank willing to provide the loan with *no personal guarantees*; then switch banks.
- Obtain equity investors to pay off the bank debt. Choose your partner carefully, and do not be unequally yoked (2 Corinthians 6:14–18).
- Another long-term option that usually works is to *lower your company's debt-to-equity ratio* and *strengthen your balance* sheet.

This can be accomplished by one of the following methods:

- Invest personal funds in the business.
- Build up any retained earnings, and leave as much profit in the company as possible.
- Implement a personal budget, and reduce your salary.
- Reduce debt by selling unnecessary assets. A common example is the use of expensive cars by business people, which is unnecessary. Replace the expensive car with a more affordable one, and use the surplus to pay down debt.

As another idea, if you're going to guarantee the debt of the corporation, have one spouse be the guarantor and let the other spouse assume title to the family home. The most important asset a family has is their home. I can affirm with conviction that God's word discourages putting your house up as security for a business loan. My advice is that you *never risk* the family home!

Over the past 45 years, I have seen too many cases where a business owner provides a personal guarantee. Then the economy goes into recession, their business loses lots of money, and the bank calls their loans and forces them into bankruptcy.

Next, the bank appoints a receiver who liquidates the assets, often at a fraction of what they're worth. The monies available are often significantly less than the bank's indebtedness. As a result, the bank forecloses on their home, and the business owner loses everything. In some cases, a marriage may break up because of the loss of the family home and financial stress, resulting in arguments and resentment between a couple.

Most Christian business owners by far are *unaware* that God's word strongly discourages personal guarantees for corporate debt. Sadly, Hosea 4:6 also holds true: "My people are destroyed from lack of knowledge." It's absolutely critical to know and follow the word of God. As Proverbs 16:3 encourages us, "Commit to the LORD whatever you do, and he will establish your plans."

Finally, if you desire God's blessing on your business and the protection of your assets, you should manage your company according to God's financial principles.

Visit www.coplandfinancialministries.org to view my seven thirty-minute videos to learn more about God's financial wisdom for business. If you are a business owner and have questions about applying biblical principles to managing your business, feel free to reach me by email at tcopland@zing-net.ca or by calling me directly at 416-818-2909.

19. Summary of Comments Regarding Questions to Consider Before Borrowing

In my experience, very few people ask the relevant biblically based financial questions (provided at the beginning of this chapter) before they borrow money. Based on my experience as a chartered professional accountant with 45 years of public accounting experience, and as a financial adviser, most people live paycheque-to-paycheque, spend all their regular income, and have no savings—not even an emergency fund. Sadly, the statistics bear this out. For example, people typically have no savings for unexpected expenditures. In addition, most fail to save for future needs, such as a down payment on a house, children's education, or a retirement fund.

In the Parable of the Tower (Luke 14:28–30), God admonishes us to plan ahead. The best way to plan financially is to create a budget that ensures you spend less than you earn so that you have a surplus to pay down debt and save for future needs.

Go to www.coplandfinancialministries.org for further information about God's word on finances and how to reduce and eliminate debt. Join one of our Zoom small groups based on my comprehensive biblical study, "Financial Management God's Way."

Also, be sure to download a copy of the Copland Budgeting System from the website and watch the thirty-minute video explaining how to develop and implement a budget. Most of the resources on the website are free.

20. Summary of Comments Regarding Co-Signing

Although the Bible discourages co-signing, remember that this is a principle and not a law. In most situations, people should *not co-sign* on someone else's loan, but there may be limited cases where co-signing is appropriate.

As an example, a father co-signs for his daughter to rent an apartment while she attends university. Practically, the father may pay for it anyway, but even if the daughter is paying and runs out of money, the father will still be able to cover the rental payments. This is one type of co-signing that I believe is appropriate.

It is not a sin to co-sign, but God warns that if you co-sign, you may suffer some negative consequences. Statistics show that the co-signer ends up paying the debt in most cases, not the borrower. That is worth considering before you co-sign for someone!

In addition, when a borrower defaults on a loan and the co-signer has to pay, their relationship is often damaged. The co-signer may resent having to pay a debt that is not theirs, and the borrower may feel embarrassed and awkward going forward with the relationship.

To learn more about co-signing, watch my two 28-minute videos on our website at www.coplandfinancialministries.org.

In addition, there are several "Financial Moments teachings" on co-signing.

V

FINANCIAL DECEPTIONS

A. OBJECTIVE OF THIS CHAPTER

To recognize some of the common financial deceptions of the world and to understand God's truth regarding specific financial issues.

B. KEY BIBLICAL PRINCIPLE

The word of God is the ultimate source of true financial wisdom.

1. Introduction

The world bombards us with many false concepts concerning finances. I call these "financial deceptions." These beliefs appear to be accurate, but are contrary to God's financial principles.

In many ways, we are engaged in a spiritual battle between the truth of God's word and the financial lies and deceptions of the world and the enemy. Satan does everything possible to mislead and deceive people in all aspects of their lives, including finances. The great news is that Jesus promised His disciples, "If you hold to my teaching, you are really my disciples. Then you will know the truth, and the truth will set you free" (John 8:31–32).

In other words, those who hold fast to the teachings of Jesus Christ will be set free from the financial deceptions of the world and Satan. When we turn to God's truth, as revealed in the Bible, we learn to manage the money

God has entrusted us according to his principles and will. In John 17:15–17, the Lord confirmed the dangers of deception from the world and Satan and the importance of knowing God's word, the ultimate source of "financial truth." Jesus said: "My prayer is not that you take them out of the world but that you protect them from the evil one. They are not of the world, even as I am not of it. Sanctify them by the truth; your word is truth."

Again, there are numerous financial deceptions, but the following are the ten most common, and each one contradicts God's word.

2. Financial Deception #1: It's Okay to Live Paycheque-to-Paycheque

Statistics reveal that most people live "paycheque-to-pay-cheque," meaning they spend all their regular income and have no surplus or savings. Sadly, most people believe this is accept-able. However, God says it is foolish. In Proverbs 21:20, the Lord said, "The wise man saves for the future, but the foolish man spends whatever he gets" (TLB).

Unfortunately, most people fall into the foolish category since they rarely save for future expenses. God's word is clear that a wise person saves for the future. Using the example of building a tower in Luke 14:28–30, Jesus demonstrates that people are foolish if they do not plan ahead and anticipate future costs.

An essential part of saving for the future is regularly putting aside enough money to cover non-monthly expenditures. For example, if your family's annual vacation costs $1,800, God's financial principles instruct you to save $150 per month over the year to afford the holiday without incurring unnecessary debt. Another example of a non-monthly expense is automobile repairs. Though these estimates may not be exact, you can generally save enough to cover your automobile repair and maintenance costs. It's also wise to have a "cushion" of at least four to eight months' worth of expenses in your savings account in the event of a significant reduction in income (for instance, if you or your spouse becomes ill or loses your job).

God's financial principles also encourage long-term saving for future needs, such as retirement and children's education. But unfortunately, history shows that most parents do not save for their children's education. As a result, many students graduate from college or university with significant debt. It is a good rule of thumb for parents to save for their children's education shortly after they are born. For example, $100 per month invested at 7 per cent will accumulate to more than $43,000 within eighteen years!

In summary, living paycheque-to-paycheque is contrary to God's word. Instead, the Bible teaches us to plan ahead and save for future needs. To accomplish this practically, the first step is to develop and implement a budget. If you need help with this, the Copland Budgeting System is available at no cost on our website: www.coplandfinancialministries.org. In addition, a thirty-minute video explains how to use the budgeting system.

3. Financial Deception #2: You Should Gain Financial Freedom Quickly

The idea of "getting rich quick" is attractive to many people. These methods include buying lottery tickets (often marketed as "Imagine the Freedom"), aggressive investing (usually accompanied by debt), and excessive hard work, which throws off one's work-life balance. However, God's instruction is different. The emphasis in Scripture is to plan and save for future needs *slowly over time.* For example, Proverbs 21:5 says, "The plans of the diligent lead to profit as surely as haste leads to poverty." In the Living Bible translation, that same Scripture reads, "Steady plodding brings prosperity; hasty speculation brings poverty." And Proverbs 13:11 says, "Whoever gathers money little by little makes it grow."

Sadly, over the past forty years, I have seen many cases where people tried to get rich quickly only to lose everything. As indicated in Proverbs 21:5, God warns that hasty decisions lead to poverty. In my experience, those who accumulated significant wealth and kept it have done so over a long period, perhaps twenty or thirty years or more.

When the book of Proverbs was written, most people were farmers who depended on their land for income. In Proverbs 28:19–20, God provided the following admonition:

> Those who work their land will have abundant food, but those who chase fantasies will have their fill of poverty. A faithful person will be richly blessed, but one eager to get rich will not go unpunished.

In short, God says that our focus should be to generate an income from our occupation or business, not from a "get rich quick" scheme. Proverbs 19:2 tells us, "Enthusiasm without knowledge is no good; haste makes mistakes" (NLT). In other words, people risky losing money when they invest or deal in areas they don't understand. God clearly warns about the dangers of trying to get rich quickly in Proverbs 23:4–5:

> Do not wear yourself out to get rich; do not trust your own cleverness. Cast but a glance at riches, and they are gone, for they will surely sprout wings and fly off to the sky like an eagle.

Further, in 1 Timothy 6:9–10, the apostle Paul outlined significant spiritual risks of chasing after riches:

Those who want to get rich fall into temptation and a trap and into many foolish and harmful desires that plunge people into ruin and destruction. For the love of money is a root of all kinds of evil. Some people, eager for money, have wandered from the faith and pierced themselves with many griefs.

It is important to note that Paul said "the love of money" is the root of all kinds of evil. Money in and of itself is not evil. Rather, it is an individual's ungodly attitude towards money and material things such as covetousness, pride, greed, selfishness, and envy. I discuss ungodly, worldly attitudes concerning money in more detail in session #11 of my book *Financial Management God's Way*, available on www.coplandfinancialministries.org.

To summarize, God's word encourages us to plan and save for future needs over time, without the wrong attitude of trying to get rich quickly. God has promised that He will meet our needs if we put Him first. In Matthew 6:31–33, Jesus said:

"Do not worry, saying, 'What shall we eat?' or 'What shall we drink?' or 'What shall we wear?' For the pagans run after all these things, and your heavenly Father knows that you need them. But seek first his kingdom and his righteousness, and all these things will be given to you as well."

4. Financial Deception #3: Debt Restructuring Solves Financial Issues

I recently counseled a man who accumulated significant credit card debt. He felt it was reasonable to restructure his debt to lower the interest rate and ensure he could make his payments.

His bank provided a line of credit at a much lower rate, which he used to pay off his credit cards.

As his financial adviser, I made sure he understood that debt restructuring treated the symptom and not the problem. The underlying issue was that he habitually spent more than he earned over the years. So, I recommended he prepare and implement a budget to ensure he had a surplus each month to pay down debt. Unfortunately, he did not follow this biblically based financial advice or change his financial habits.

Several years later, he maxed out his credit cards and personal line of credit again. His only option was to take out a second mortgage on his house to pay off a mountain of debt. Again, I encouraged him to develop and implement a budget so he would spend less than he earned to have a surplus to pay off his debt. Unfortunately, he did not listen to my advice, and the same problem arose four years later.

His credit sources were now depleted, and he was forced to withdraw money from his retirement plan to settle his high-interest credit card debt and satisfy his creditors. Two problems emerged: First, the withdrawal of his retirement funds resulted in a tax liability; second, there was concern that he would not have sufficient funds for retirement.

At this point, you may think this individual was not very astute financially. The opposite is true! He was a professional accountant who understood and agreed with my advice. However, he was unwilling to make the necessary sacrifices to reduce his spending and alter his lifestyle.

Consequently, he experienced significant financial hardship because he failed to follow God's financial principles. Further, he did not follow the instruction in James 1:22, which says, "Do not merely listen to the word, and so deceive yourselves. Do what it says."

5. Financial Difficulties Can Reflect an Underlying Spiritual Problem

It's important to mention that financial difficulties often reflect underlying spiritual problems. In other words, financial problems can be rooted in spiritual issues that extend beyond the financial realm. For example, heart issues like greed, covetousness, lack of contentment, selfishness, or pride can lead to financial difficulties. These mindsets are contrary to the word of God.

What is the solution? I believe the answer is to meditate on God's word concerning finances. Then you will begin to adopt the "mind of Christ" and think differently about money and material things. Romans 12:2 says, "Do not conform to the pattern of this world, but be transformed by the renewing of your mind." And how do you renew your mind? Joshua 1:8 answers: "Keep this Book of the Law always on your lips; meditate on it day and night, so that you may be careful to do everything written in it. Then you will be prosperous and successful."

6. If You Are in Debt, I Urge You to Do Two Things

1. Develop and implement a budget to ensure you spend less than you earn, then use the surplus to pay off debt. You can obtain a copy of my Excel-based budgeting template from our website, www.coplandfinancialministries.org for free. Also, a thirty-minute video explains how to use it.
2. Study and meditate on God's word regularly regarding finances. One of the best ways to do this is to participate in our twelve-week in-depth Bible study, "Financial Management God's Way." This program has seen significant and permanent transformations in how people think about and manage money.

Please go to our website to watch our online interactive version, or join one of our Zoom groups. Ideally, I encourage you to purchase a copy of my workbook, *Financial Management God's Way.*

7. Financial Deception #4: More Money Brings Happiness

There is a common misconception that having lots of money will make you happy. This is a financial deception. Even though additional income can ease financial pressures (if one manages their money well), it does not bring happiness in and of itself. Certainly, money cannot provide the joy and peace that only God can give!

Ecclesiastes 5:10 gives a glimpse into the human heart: "Whoever loves money never has enough; whoever loves wealth is never satisfied with their income."

I've seen many individuals and couples with significant wealth who lacked joy and peace. For example, I recall a husband and wife who started with nothing and accumulated around fifty million dollars' worth of assets. Yet despite their extraordinary wealth, their unhappiness was evident to anyone who knew them. They were plagued by concerns such as "What if we lose our money?" and "How should we invest?" Furthermore, they often quarreled with each other, their children, and their employees.

Stress and anxiety hindered their ability to experience the peace of God, which transcends all understanding (Philippians 4:7). Only God can bring genuine peace, joy, and happiness through his Holy Spirit. In John 14:26–27, Jesus said:

> "The Advocate, the Holy Spirit, whom the Father will send in my name, will teach you all things and will remind you of everything I have said to you. Peace I leave with you; my peace I give you. I do not give to you as the world

gives. Do not let your hearts be troubled and do not be afraid."

Many affluent Christians do not experience God's joy and peace. Rather, they struggle with anger, frustration, weariness, and even depression. Remember, "The fruit of the Spirit is love, joy, peace, forbearance, kindness, goodness, faithfulness, gentleness, and self-control" (Galatians 5:22–23). If you feel weary and burdened, I encourage you to accept Jesus Christ's invitation in Matthew 11:28–30:

> "Come to me, all you who are weary and burdened, and I will give you rest. Take my yoke upon you and learn from me, for I am gentle and humble in heart, and you will find rest for your souls. For my yoke is easy and my burden is light."

Having worked with wealthy clients in my accounting practice and ministry, I believe that the key to happiness isn't more money but rather a close, personal relationship with God. In John 15, Jesus described this level of intimacy as "abiding," which means continually being in communion with God, not just on Sunday mornings or special occasions.

To learn more about abiding in Christ, I recommend you read *Secrets of the Vine* by Dr. Bruce Wilkinson (Multnomah Books, 2001). According to the author, God prunes us so that our lives reflect Christ and have a more significant impact for eternity. I have read it several times. It is an excellent book!

8. Financial Deception #5: "Buy Now and Pay Later" Makes Sense

Today, you can purchase almost anything with little or no down payment—automobiles, furniture, boats, and snowmobiles! It is common to see advertisements that entice people to buy with financing deals like "no payments and no interest" for one or two years.

Nowadays, getting credit is almost effortless. To worsen matters, banks often encourage homeowners to take out a line of credit against their home's increased value and equity. The availability of easy credit creates a strong temptation to buy now and pay later. As a result, many purchase items on credit that they cannot afford or really do not need.

In contrast to the world's way of doing things, God's directive is to wait for His provision and perfect timing. Psalm 37:7 states, "Rest in the LORD and wait patiently for Him" (NASB). Likewise, Lamentations 3:24 reminds us, "The LORD is my portion; therefore I will wait for him."

I know many cases where Christians have prayed and asked God to meet a particular need. For example, several years ago, a Christian couple with a modest income needed another vehicle because theirs was breaking down. So first, they prayed and asked God to meet this specific need, and then they *waited patiently* for His divine provision.

I don't believe it was a coincidence when someone at their church gave them a used van in excellent condition! Because they waited and trusted God for His provision, He blessed them and provided in a way that brought Him glory. He is awesome!

If you have a need, I encourage you to pray and wait for God to answer. There are many ways God can provide—such as an unexpected income or gift, a better deal, or a less costly alternative. Unfortunately, many do not pray and wait for God's unique provision. Instead, the temptation to "buy now and pay later" is too great, so they often buy what they want without consulting God and waiting patiently for the Lord's provision. As a result,

God is deprived of the opportunity to provide for their needs, ultimately for His glory.

As promised in Matthew 6:31–33, God will meet our needs as long as we put Him first and manage our finances according to His biblical principles and specific will. The apostle Paul said in Philippians 4:19, "My God will meet all your needs according to the riches of his glory in Christ Jesus." Note that God has promised to meet our needs, not necessarily our wants and desires. God has also instructed us in Hebrews 13:5 to be content with what He has provided: "Keep your lives free from the love of money and be content with what you have, because God has said, 'Never will I leave you; never will I forsake you.'"

In summary, God has promised to meet our needs, but He desires that we wait for His provision and timing. This is a very different approach, unlike the world's mindset to buy now and pay later.

9. Financial Deception #6: Smart People Use Other People's Money

Many people believe it is sound financial thinking to borrow money to invest to make a lot more money. In other words, they believe the financial deception that "smart people use other people's money," not their own. This is a lie from the world and Satan. The only way that could be true is if you could predict the future—that is, could know with certainty the direction of the markets and economy.

The biblical truth is that only God knows the future. Though people can make their best guesses about the future, they are frequently wrong. Throughout the past century, no one has been able to predict the markets' direction consistently.

For example, between 1993 and 2000, the value of most stocks in Canada and the United States increased significantly. As a result of false confidence, many used other people's money—they borrowed capital intending to increase their returns. However, from 2000 to 2002, shares traded on the Toronto and New York exchanges decreased by about 50 per cent, on average. Many who borrowed money to bolster their investments lost tons of money. Some not only lost their initial capital but ended up with a deficit since the value of their stocks dropped below what they borrowed.

The same principle applies to real estate. During the middle to the late 1980s, real estate values in Toronto increased significantly. Many believed they would never decline. However, the values dropped drastically between 1990 and 1995. Commercial real estate decreased by about 75 per cent and residential real estate by 25–50 per cent, depending on the property. Those who had a lot of debt were hurt badly, and some lost their business, home, or investment property. The same thing happened during the 2008 to 2009 recession.

As of writing this book, the most recent example is the bear market that occurred as a result of the COVID-19 pandemic in February and March 2020. On average, stocks declined by 32 per cent within a month, and those who invested using debt lost a great deal of money. Most of those who used debt were forced to sell when the market was down, which is the exact opposite of what you want to do.

Many businesses try to use debt to their advantage. There may be periods when they benefit as they expand faster than they otherwise would, but in due course, every business will experience financial challenges. Companies with a lot of debt will suffer the most during tough times, such as a recession, forcing some into bankruptcy.

The biblical truth is that we do not know what will happen tomorrow. Proverbs 27:1 says, "Do not boast about tomorrow, for you do not know what a day may bring." In other words, there are no "sure deals." The same principle applies in business. James 4:13–15 warns:

> Now listen, you who say, "Today or tomorrow we will go to this or that city, spend a year there, carry on business and make money." Why, you do not even know what will happen tomorrow … Instead, you ought to say, "If it is the Lord's will, we will live and do this or that."

Ultimately, no one knows what will happen tomorrow. Only God knows what the future holds. As a result, we should use minimal debt for investments and business expansion or ideally carry no debt. Overall, a central theme of God's word is that He advises us to have minimal to no debt, not maximum debt.

10. Financial Deception #7: A Lot of Money Equals Financial Freedom

People often believe that financial freedom can only be achieved when they have a lot of money and material things. This is a deception from the world and the enemy. God warned, "Whoever loves money never has enough; whoever loves wealth is never satisfied with their income. This too is meaningless" (Ecclesiastes 5:10).

Many wealthy people have no peace in the area of finances. In other words, they are by no means financially free. Instead, they are often stressed by money-related issues, like "How should I invest my money?" "What if I lose my money?" In some cases, they may be workaholics with an unquenchable desire to accumulate more and more. As a result, anxiety, and worry dominate their minds when it comes to money matters.

The only way to achieve true financial freedom is to have God's peace and joy in the area of finances. To gain His peace and joy in your finances, consider the following:

- Believe that God's truth is your only defense against the deceptions in this world. It is His truth that will set you free. Jesus said, "If you hold to my teaching, you are really my disciples. Then you will know the truth, and the truth will set you free" (John 8:31–32).
- Recognize God's truth that we are stewards of what He has entrusted to us. The word *steward* most closely translates from the Greek to mean "manager"—a manager is responsible for taking care of something on behalf of someone else. Further, Psalm 24:1 reminds us, "The earth is the Lord's, and everything in it, the world, and all who live in it." Remember, God owns everything (Haggai 2:8). It is our responsibility to manage the money and material things God has given us, by learning and applying His financial principles and fulfilling His will for our lives.
- When you manage your finances God's way, you can "cast your cares on the Lord" (Psalm 55:22) and trust Him to meet your needs (Proverbs 3:5–6). You will then experience and enjoy God's perfect peace in your finances, which will often extend to your relationships as well.
- With the Lord's help, learn to be content with God's provision. The apostle Paul said: "I have learned to be content whatever the circumstances. I know what it is to be in need, and I know what it is to have plenty. I have learned the secret of being content in any and every situation, whether well fed or hungry, whether living in plenty or in want. I can do all this through him who gives me strength" (Philippians 4:11–13).
- Acknowledge that the accumulation of money and material things are temporary and of no eternal value (Matthew

6:19–21). According to God's truth, a selfish desire to accumulate wealth and material things is of no value from an eternal perspective.

- Experience the joy of giving, by giving generously as the Lord leads. Jesus said, "It is more blessed to give than to receive" (Acts 20:35). Giving with a cheerful heart and out of love for God enables you to experience the joy of giving and to be free of the love of money.
- Prayerfully ask God to give you His wisdom in managing money and His peace, particularly in the area of finances. In John 14:27, Jesus said, "Peace I leave with you; my peace I give you. I do not give to you as the world gives. Do not let your hearts be troubled and do not be afraid."

In summary, one of the deceptions of this world is that financial freedom comes from having lots of money and material possessions. The key to true financial freedom is having an intimate relationship with God and managing His money according to His ways. If you do this, you will experience genuine joy, peace, and contentment from the Lord.

11. Financial Deception #8: Bankruptcy Solves Financial Problems

People in financial difficulty often believe that declaring bankruptcy is the best option to solve their financial problems. Unfortunately, bankruptcy only treats the symptom. Based on statistics and my experience, most bankrupt people get into financial difficulty again within ten years! This is generally because the root of the problem is the violation of God's financial principles, which often continues even if current debts are eliminated.

The Bible is clear that it is not God's will for anyone to go bankrupt. As Psalm 37:21 states, "The wicked borrow and do not repay, but the righteous give generously." In other words, not paying your debts is a sin.

On the other hand, it is implied that a righteous person pays what is owed and goes "the extra mile" by giving generously, even where there is no obligation to do so. Further, what kind of a "light into a world of darkness" is a Christian who declares bankruptcy? In Matthew 5:14–16, Jesus said:

> "You are the light of the world. A town built on a hill cannot be hidden. Neither do people light a lamp and put it under a bowl. Instead they put it on its stand, and it gives light to everyone in the house. In the same way, let your light shine before others, that they may see your good deeds and glorify your Father in heaven."

The point is that declaring bankruptcy is not a good testimony for a Christian! Therefore, I believe God does not want His children to go bankrupt.

If you face financial difficulty, develop and follow a budget, and learn to implement God's financial principles. These would include praying for God's wisdom (James 1:5) and His specific direction (Psalm 32:8), obtaining biblical financial counsel (Psalm 1:1–3), and meditating on key Scriptures (Joshua 1:8) with respect to finances to allow God, through His word (Hebrews 4:12), to change the way you think about and manage money (Romans 12:2). If you do this, you will manage money in a biblical fashion. And remember, God has promised He will meet your needs (Matthew 6:31–33), but not necessarily your wants and desires.

Since 1982, I have had the privilege of counseling over 10,000 people in severe financial difficulty. When individuals learned and implemented God's financial principles, God blessed them in unusual ways and almost always enabled them to avoid bankruptcy.

12. What If You Have Already Declared Bankruptcy?

If you have already declared bankruptcy, may I encourage you in several ways:

- God loves you, and He will forgive the act of bankruptcy if you sincerely confess that sin to the Lord. First John 1:9 reassures us, "If we confess our sins, he is faithful and just and will forgive us our sins and purify us from all unrighteousness."
- Depend upon the Holy Spirit and God's wisdom from His word to bring you through this financial hardship. Ask God to reveal the root cause(s) of your financial difficulties that may have led to bankruptcy. The reality is that most Christians violate God's financial principles, often unknowingly. Or perhaps they have an ungodly attitude or mindset about money that needs to change. Therefore, it is critical to study and meditate on God's word regarding your finances so that you have the "mind of Christ" (1 Corinthians 2:16) to manage the money God has entrusted to you. You can find helpful resources at www.coplandfinancialministries.org. Most are available at no cost.
- Develop and implement a budget to ensure you spend less than you earn every month to have a surplus for non-monthly and unexpected expenditures. Simply, a budget is a useful tool for practical short-term and long-term financial planning.

In summary, another deception of this world is that bankruptcy can solve one's financial problems. But unfortunately, bankruptcy usually only treats the symptoms. Generally, the root cause of one's financial difficulties is a violation of one or more biblical principles.

13. Financial Deception #9: Faith-Filled Christians Will Enjoy Prosperity

Many people believe the "prosperity gospel," that if you are a Christian with sufficient faith in God, and if you ask God to bless you abundantly, then God is obligated to bless you with lots of money and material things. And if you're not wealthy, your faith must be weak. None of these are true, nor are they biblical. They are financial deceptions!

Scripture contains many examples of committed believers who had incredible faith and trust in the Lord, yet they were not blessed with financial wealth. The following examples illustrate this.

First, Jesus Christ, our Lord and Saviour, could have lived a lavish lifestyle, but He did not. In Luke 9:58, Jesus said, "Foxes have dens and birds have nests, but the Son of Man has no place to lay his head." In other words, Jesus did not own a house. Even though He was the Son of God, there is no indication that God provided Him with material wealth.

Another example is when Jesus made His triumphant entry into Jerusalem on a "borrowed donkey" (Matthew 21:7), thus fulfilling the prophecy in Zechariah 9:9. The Scriptures reveal that Jesus lived a modest lifestyle, even though He was the King of kings and the Lord of lords—the God of the universe! Clearly, Jesus did not have a prosperity gospel mindset!

Second, the apostle Paul, who wrote more than half of the New Testament, had few material possessions. In Philippians 4:11–13, Paul said:

> I am not saying this because I am in need, for I have learned to be content whatever the circumstances. I know what it is to be in need, and I know what it is to have plenty. I have learned the secret of being content in any and every situation, whether well fed or hungry, whether

living in plenty or in want. I can do all this through him who gives me strength.

Paul emphasized the importance of learning to be content with whatever God provides. We can all learn to be satisfied with God's provision by relying on the Lord Jesus Christ and focusing on things of eternal value rather than our temporal concerns. In Colossians 3:1–2, Paul wrote:

Since, then, you have been raised with Christ, set your hearts on things above, where Christ is, seated at the right hand of God. Set your minds on things above, not on earthly things.

In other words, focus on things of eternal value, such as the salvation of others, discipleship, and evangelism. And "the peace of God, which transcends all understanding, will guard your hearts and minds in Christ Jesus" (Philippians 4:7) and enable you to be content with His financial provision.

Third, John the Baptist was a great man of God. He was the prophet who predicted the coming of the Messiah and the man who baptized Jesus. Yet every indication in Scripture shows he had a very modest lifestyle. Of interest, in Luke 3:14, he told some soldiers, "Be content with your pay."

These are examples of godly men who did not have tremendous wealth, including the Lord Himself! So, it is a mistake to assume that God will bless a person with wealth if they are a devoted Christian with enough faith. God may bless His children financially, and He often does, especially if they manage their money according to biblical principles and give generously to God's work (Luke 6:38; 2 Corinthians 9:6–7).

However, no matter how faithful or wise a Christian is with their finances, wealth is not guaranteed. One guarantee God does give is that if you manage your money according to His financial principles, He will meet your needs. As Paul says in Philippians 4:19, "My God will meet all your needs according to the riches of his glory in Christ Jesus."

As a final note, God promises eternal rewards in heaven to those who manage money his way and give generously to his work. In Matthew 16:27, Jesus said, "For the Son of Man is going to come in his Father's glory with his angels, and then he will reward each person according to what they have done."

14. Financial Deception #10: "Step Out in Faith" and Trust God for the Payments

Often when a Christian plans to purchase a major item that requires significant debt, such as a house or a car, someone will encourage them to "step out in faith," buy the item, take on the debt, and "trust God for the payments." If borrowing and buying something is an act of stepping out in faith, then non-Christians do it all the time too! It doesn't take faith to borrow and buy anything.

It does require a great deal of faith to trust God and wait patiently for him to provide the cash or a better alternative. Psalm 37:7 states, "Be still before the LORD and wait patiently for him." And when it comes to the purchase of a home, God's word instructs us to wait until we have a substantial down payment to assume a mortgage we can comfortably afford.

In other words, even before you purchase a home, prepare a budget that includes your future mortgage payment, utilities, property taxes, repairs, and maintenance costs. In this way, you ensure you will have a surplus each month for unexpected expenses (Proverbs 21:20). It is never a good idea to take on a mortgage that you cannot afford to repay!

C. SUMMARY OF THE TEN FINANCIAL DECEPTIONS

Although there are other financial deceptions in the world, the following are the most common:

Deception #1: It's Okay to Live Paycheque-to-Paycheque

Deception #2: You Should Gain Financial Freedom Quickly

Deception #3: Debt Restructuring Solves Financial Issues

Deception #4: More Money Brings Happiness

Deception #5: "Buy Now and Pay Later" Makes Sense

Deception #6: Smart People Use Other People's Money

Deception #7: A Lot of Money Equals Financial Freedom

Deception #8: Bankruptcy Solves Financial Problems

Deception #9: Faith-Filled Christians Will Enjoy Prosperity

Deception #10: "Step Out in Faith" and Trust God for the Payments

D. RECOMMENDED MEMORY VERSES FOR DEALING WITH FINANCIAL DECEPTIONS

"Do not conform to the pattern of this world, but be transformed by the renewing of your mind" (Romans 12:2).

"Keep this Book of the Law always on your lips; meditate on it day and night, so that you may be careful to do everything written in it. Then you will be prosperous and successful" (Joshua 1:8).

"To the Jews who had believed him, Jesus said, 'If you hold to my teaching, you are really my disciples. Then you will know the truth, and the truth will set you free'" (John 8:31–32).

Here's a challenge for you! For the next thirty days, I encourage you to meditate on the above three Scriptures daily, and allow God to start transforming the way you think about and manage money.

E. CASE STUDIES, QUESTIONS, TOM'S COMMENTS

15. Case Study #1: A Couple Did Not Save for Retirement

Bob and Joan are married and in their sixties with two grown children. Both became Christians as teenagers. Over the past thirty-five years, Bob earned an above-average income, and Joan worked part-time. They plan to retire within three years.

The couple consults a financial adviser for the first time to ensure their finances are in order. The financial adviser informs Bob and Joan that they do not have enough money to retire. Rather, they must both work for another fourteen years to save several hundred dollars per month before they can afford to retire. They are surprised and disappointed to learn they must delay retirement that long.

As they reflect, they realize they have lived paycheque-to-paycheque, accumulating debt instead of paying it off. They did not diligently save for retirement or health care costs. Further, Bob was recently diagnosed with health issues, and though they are not life-threatening, his doctor recommends he only work part-time to slow down and rest more. However, Bob knows he has no choice but to work full-time to pay off debt and save for retirement.

When they contemplate the reality of their situation, Bob suggests they borrow a substantial amount against the equity of their home to invest in "growth stocks." The goal is to earn higher returns than usual, allowing them to retire earlier. Joan, on the other hand, is uncomfortable with the risk associated with putting their home up for security.

Please consider the following questions and write your answers before you read my comments.

QUESTION #1
What financial deceptions did Bob and Joan likely believe and follow over the past thirty-five years. Please provide a Scripture reference for each.

TOM'S COMMENT
The following is a list of financial deceptions that Bob and Joan believed.

- Bob and Joan believed the lie that living paycheque-to-paycheque is okay, evidenced by the fact that they spent all of their regular income. They also failed to save for long-term needs, such as retirement and health care costs (Proverbs 21:20).
- Due to their credit card debt, they probably believed the financial deception that buying now and paying later made sense. God instructs us to "wait patiently for him" (Psalm 37:7) and "be content with what you have" (Hebrews 13:5).
- As they had a personal line of credit, they likely believed the deception that debt restructuring would solve their financial problems (Proverbs 14:15).
- Bob believed the lie that "smart people use other people's money," as he is willing to risk the equity of their home to invest in stocks so they can retire earlier.
- In the Parable of the Tower in Luke 14:28–30, Christ advised us to plan ahead and considered it foolish not to do so. It is

unfortunate that Bob and Joan fell into the foolish category and are now suffering the long-term consequences.

QUESTION #2

If you were Bob and Joan's financial adviser, what biblically based financial advice would you give them? Please provide a Scripture reference for each point.

TOM'S COMMENT

Prayer is the first step. Prayerfully seek God for His wisdom (James 1:5) and His specific guidance. Psalm 25:12 states, "Who, then, are those who fear the LORD? He will instruct them in the ways they should choose." Bob and Joan did not ask God for wisdom and direction, and as a result, they experienced a financial crisis. Here's what they need to do:

- Confess the sin of violating many of God's financial principles. First John 1:8–9 says, "If we claim to be without sin, we deceive ourselves and the truth is not in us. If we confess our sins, he is faithful and just and will forgive us our sins and purify us from all unrighteousness."
- Learn about God's financial principles by participating in my in-depth biblical study, "Financial Management God's Way." God, through His word, will direct them to manage money wisely (Psalm 119:105).

- Change the way they think about finances (Romans 12:2) by meditating on appropriate Scriptures (Joshua 1:8).
- With God's help, learn to be content with a reduced lifestyle (Philippians 4:11–13). This point is crucial since it's obvious from their accumulated debt that, as a couple with above-average incomes, they have been living a lifestyle that is beyond their means.
- Develop and implement a budget (Luke 14:28–30) to ensure they spend less than they earn each month, have sufficient funds to pay down debt and provide for future needs, like retirement.
- Regularly study God's financial principles in His word (Psalm 119:1–11; 2 Timothy 3:16–17). Whatever they do, they must not borrow against the equity in their house to invest in stocks! This clearly violates Scripture. Yet over the years, I have seen many people attempt to make up for previous financial mistakes by doing this. Unfortunately, the outcome is often disastrous, as most people experience substantial losses instead of profits. The biblical way is to develop and implement a budget (Luke 14:28–30), to ensure they have a surplus each month to pay down debt and save for retirement. Once their debts are paid off then they should invest their surplus funds into a diversified portfolio in accordance with Ecclesiastes 11:2.
- Another benefit would be to do the "dollar-cost averaging" method by investing a certain amount each month over a long period, which is consistent with Scripture. Proverbs 21:5 (TLB) states, "Steady plodding brings prosperity; hasty speculation brings poverty."

QUESTION #3

What impact do you think Bob and Joan's money management had on their children? Assuming both children went to university, what about the funding of their children's education? And what impact could it have indirectly on their grandchildren?

TOM'S COMMENT

Bob and Joan were deceived by many financial deceptions and managed their money according to the world's standards rather than God's. Sadly, their children are likely to follow the same path. Proverbs 22:6 states, "Start children off on the way they should go, and even when they are old they will not turn from it." Without realizing it, Bob and Joan set a bad example for their children.

Additionally, since Bob and Joan lived paycheque-to-paycheque, spent all of their regular income, accumulated significant debt, and failed to save for retirement, they were unlikely to save for their children's education. Unfortunately, their children are at risk of following their parents' bad example by using credit freely. Therefore, they may finish post-secondary education with significant debt and accumulate even more debt once they start working. If Bob and Joan's children manage money according to worldly standards, their worldly financial habits will likely be passed on to their children—in other words, Bob and Joan's grandchildren.

My intention is not to be mean but rather to *speak the truth in love* to those reading this book. Parents must teach their children how to handle money in God's way, not the world's way. According to Deuteronomy 5:9 and Numbers 14:18, the parents' sins can be passed on to the third and fourth generations. I have seen many instances in which parents' worldly financial habits have been unintentionally passed down generationally to their children, grandchildren, and even great-grandchildren. From my heart, I sincerely encourage you to learn and apply what the Bible says about finances, teach your children and grandchildren, and lead by a godly example.

QUESTION #4

What biblically based advice should Bob and Joan give to their adult children? Provide a reference to Scripture.

TOM'S COMMENT

Bob and Joan would be wise to humble themselves (Proverbs 22:4) and explain their financial mistakes to their adult children. In doing so, they can help their children keep from making similar mistakes and encourage them to follow the wisdom of God's word regarding finances (Psalm 1:1–3; 119:24). Indeed, any financial knowledge gained by their children will be beneficial to their future grandchildren.

Additionally, Bob and Joan should advise their children to develop and implement a budget and save for their future needs (Luke 14:28–30), such as retirement, health-care costs, and their grandchildren's education. Further, Bob and Joan could explain the importance of operating with minimal debt to avoid being a "slave to the lender" (Proverbs 22:7). In addition, they could encourage them to seek God's guidance regarding their finances through his word (1 Kings 22:5), and learn to be content with the income God provides (Hebrews 13:5).

QUESTION #5

What is the relevance and application of the following verses for Bob and Joan's situation? Write your comments below in each verse.

"The wise man saves for the future, but the foolish man spends whatever he gets" (Proverbs 21:20, TLB).

TOM'S COMMENT

Bob and Joan fall into the foolish category because they spent whatever income they received and did not save for future needs.

"Suppose one of you wants to build a tower. Won't you first sit down and estimate the cost to see if you have enough money to complete it? For if you lay the foundation and are not able to finish it, everyone who sees it will ridicule you, saying, 'This person began to build and wasn't able to finish'" (Luke 14:28–30).

TOM'S COMMENT

While we no longer "build towers," most people want to build retirement funds and education funds for their children. Jesus said that if you don't plan to ensure you have enough money, you are foolish. Unfortunately, Bob and Joan did not plan their finances with saving and investing in mind to ensure they could afford retirement as planned.

"Your word is a lamp for my feet, a light on my path" (Psalm 119:105).

TOM'S COMMENT

In God's word, we can gain insight into how to manage money to plan and provide for our future. In cases where there are several options within biblical guidelines, God can highlight specific Scriptures that will guide a Christian through prayer and reading His word through the Holy Spirit.

"In fact, though by this time you ought to be teachers, you need someone to teach you the elementary truths of God's word all over again. You need milk, not solid food! Anyone who lives on milk, being still an infant, is not acquainted with the teaching about righteousness. But solid food is for the mature, who by constant use have trained themselves to distinguish good from evil" (Hebrews 5:12–14).

TOM'S COMMENT

Given that Bob and Joan were Christians for a long time, it would be reasonable for them to be familiar with God's financial management principles. In this stage of their lives, they should be teaching others how to manage money according to God's word. Unfortunately, that is not the case. Instead, Bob and Joan need someone to teach them what God's word says on finances.

Of interest, Bob and Joan's situation is quite common. Many Bible-believing, Spirit-filled Christians are spiritually mature overall, except in the area of finances! Since they have little or no knowledge of God's financial principles, they manage money according to the patterns of the world. For instance, I know of many pastors, elders, and deacons and others in leadership positions who have incredible spiritual gifts and talents. Still, quite a few of them violate biblical financial principles unknowingly.

16. Case Study #2: A Couple Covet What Others Have

Jack and Sue have three children and are members of a Bible-based church. They often notice and desire the material possessions of others and frequently make purchases on credit. Jack is proud of his boat and luxurious automobile, and Sue boasts of their new home with upscale furnishings and decor.

Not surprisingly, over the past sixteen years of their marriage, Jack and Sue have experienced financial stress. For example, twelve years ago, they owed $25,000 on their credit cards and could not afford the monthly minimum payments. However, after meeting with their banker, he explained that he could solve their problem by offering them a "debt consolidation loan" with a lower interest rate and five-year payment term.

A few years later, the finance company threatened to reclaim the couple's two expensive automobiles. To pay off their car loans, they took out a second mortgage on their house with a twenty-five-year amortization. Today, Jack and Sue have "maxed out" all of their credit cards and personal line of credit. They have also borrowed the maximum amount against the value of their home. Furthermore, they have overdue loans from their parents and several church members.

Jack and Sue have a poor credit rating as they have missed several loan payments. They argue about money almost daily, so the likelihood of separation or divorce is high. Jack and Sue feel their financial debt is insurmountable. They conclude that their best course of action would be to declare bankruptcy to eliminate their debt, solve their financial problems, and preserve their marriage.

QUESTION #1

Please list the financial deceptions that Jack and Sue likely believed and followed over the years. Provide a reference to Scripture.

TOM'S COMMENT

Jack and Sue likely believed the following financial deceptions.

- They believed the lie that debt restructuring would solve their financial problems (Proverbs 14:15). This is evidenced by the fact that they restructured their debt a few times but still had financial difficulties.
- They had credit card debt, car loan payments, and loans owing to family and friends. This indicates they believed the lie that it makes sense to "buy now and pay later", when they should have learned to wait upon the Lord for His provision (Lamentations 3:24).
- Although they had not yet declared bankruptcy, they believed the lie that bankruptcy would solve their financial problems.

QUESTION #2

Did Jack and Sue struggle with any ungodly attitudes? If so, please provide a Scripture reference for each.

TOM'S COMMENT

- Jack and Sue noticed and desired other people's material possessions. This is covetousness (Exodus 20:17) and an ungodly attitude.
- Jack and Sue struggled with pride (Proverbs 21:4), as they felt superior to others because of their material possessions.
- They were not content with God's provision, spending beyond the income God gave them (1 Timothy 6:6–8).

QUESTION #3

If you were Jack and Sue's financial adviser, what biblically based financial advice would you give them? Provide a Scripture reference for each point.

TOM'S COMMENT

Here are some biblical financial tips for Jack and Sue:

- First, pray and ask God for His wisdom and guidance (James 1:5).
- Confess the sin of violating many of God's financial principles (1 John 1:9).

- Attend our in-depth biblical financial study, "Financial Management God's Way." This study is where we have seen the most significant and permanent changes in the way people manage money. By His word, God directs people through many Scriptures (Psalm 119:105).
- Renew the way they think about finances (Romans 12:2) by meditating upon the appropriate Scriptures (Joshua 1:8).
- With God's help, learn to be content with a reduced lifestyle (Philippians 4:11–13).
- Develop and implement a budget (Luke 14:28–30) to ensure they spend less than they earn each month, save sufficient funds to pay down debt, and provide for future needs.
- Regularly study God's financial principles in His word (Psalm 119:1–11).
- They need to put God first (Matthew 6:31–33) in managing the money that God has entrusted to them. In other words, use their money in a way that is consistent with God's principles and will.

QUESTION #4

Do you think Jack and Sue should declare bankruptcy? Will it solve their financial problems? After all, it will eliminate their debts and give them a fresh start. Please provide appropriate references to Scripture.

TOM'S COMMENT

No. Despite today's laws, bankruptcy is still a sin in God's eyes (Psalm 37:21) and a bad witness to non-Christians. After all, what kind of a "light of the world" (Matthew 5:14–16) are Christians who do not pay their debts?

Jack and Sue are unlikely to have much success in witnessing to a non-Christian lender when they haven't met their financial obligations. If Jack and Sue go bankrupt, they will no longer be a credible witness for Christ to their creditors.

Bankruptcy will not solve Jack and Sue's financial problems, as it will only treat the symptom of excessive debt. The underlying cause of their financial problems is that they have violated many biblical financial principles and believed many lies from the world and Satan. They will likely get into financial trouble again if they declare bankruptcy, as their ungodly attitude and unbiblical approach to money management will likely continue.

QUESTION #5

If Jack and Sue separate due to financial stress, would that justify them declaring bankruptcy with the hope of preserving their marriage? Write your answer below, and provide a reference to Scripture.

TOM'S COMMENT

Generally, no, since they will end up in financial trouble again if they fail to deal with the underlying cause of the problem, which is not following biblical financial principles. Therefore, their highest priority is to learn and apply God's word concerning finances.

Furthermore, if they separate and have two places to pay for, they will be far worse off financially. According to Proverbs

22:3, "The prudent see danger and take refuge, but the simple continue and pay the penalty."

17. If You Are Forced into Bankruptcy by a Creditor

I have seen situations where people have been forced into bankruptcy by their creditors, and I believe there is a difference. When a creditor or bank takes legal action and forces an individual into bankruptcy, and if that person has done all they can to avoid the bankruptcy, then I believe that will be different biblically and spiritually from a person who initiates bankruptcy to avoid their financial obligations.

Often people file for bankruptcy because they do not want to assume responsibility for their debts, and they do not want to learn to be content with less and apply biblical financial principles to get out of debt.

Please read the following Scriptures, and discuss their relevance and application with respect to Jack and Sue's situation. Then write your comments below each verse.

"The simple believe anything, but the prudent give thought to their steps" (Proverbs 14:15).

TOM'S COMMENT

Jack and Sue trusted the advice of their banker (that the debt consolidation loan would solve their financial problems). They did not give any thought to the real cause of their indebtedness (that they habitually spent more than they earned and accumulated debt).

"Let no debt remain outstanding, except the continuing debt to love one another, for whoever loves others has fulfilled the law" (Romans 13:8).

TOM'S COMMENT

They did not follow the admonition in these Scriptures, as they consistently failed to pay their debt obligations on time and accumulated debt. As you can see in the above Scripture, the non-payment of one's debts is contrasted with the "fulfillment of the law" by loving one's neighbor. Therefore, when Christians do not pay debts, they are *not* demonstrating God's love. But he gives us more grace. That is why Scripture says:

> "God opposes the proud but shows favor to the humble." Submit yourselves, then, to God. Resist the devil, and he will flee from you. Come near to God and he will come near to you … Humble yourselves before the Lord, and he will lift you up. (James 4:6–8, 10)

TOM'S COMMENT

Jack and Sue have a problem with pride. They believe that their material assets make them better than others. This ungodly attitude reflects a significant spiritual problem. They need to spend quality time with the Lord in prayer, asking God to humble them.

In addition, they should meditate on Scriptures that emphasize the importance of humility, such as Daniel 4:37, 1 Peter 5:5–6, and Proverbs 16:5. God will bless them in due time if they do this.

"Godliness with contentment is great gain. For we brought nothing into the world, and we can take nothing out of it. But if we have food and clothing, we will be content with that" (1 Timothy 6:6–8).

TOM'S COMMENT

Jack and Sue need to understand the biblical truth that what matters from God's perspective is godliness and contentment, not the acquisition of material things. They must learn to be content with God's provision of their needs (Philippians 4:11–13), which is unlikely to include their wants and desires.

> "You are the light of the world. A town built on a hill cannot be hidden. Neither do people light a lamp and put it under a bowl. Instead, they put it on its stand, and it gives light to everyone in the house. In the same way, let your light shine before others, that they may see your good deeds and glorify your Father in heaven" (Matthew 5:14–16).

TOM'S COMMENT

As a result of their poor money management, Jack and Sue have not been a godly testimony as they have not met their financial obligations. Jack and Sue believed in Satan's lies and violated God's financial principles.

They need to understand that they have been a bad witness to non-believers, a discouragement to fellow believers, and a bad example for them. It is absolutely essential they start managing money according to God's principles and God's will.

18. Case Study #3: An Individual Learns Biblical Principles of Investing

George spent considerable time studying the stock market and reading numerous investment newsletters during his twenties. He was confident that using debt would substantially increase his returns. George wanted to build a large portfolio to be "financially free" by the time he was thirty. He told his pastor that he would make significant donations to his church once he accomplished this goal.

Unfortunately, his investments and the markets did not increase in value as he anticipated but dropped in value instead. As a result, he lost his original capital and ended up with a deficit. George was forced to find a second job in order to pay off his debt, and his involvement in the church ceased as a result. George grew disappointed with God when he could not understand why he was not financially blessed.

During his thirties, George studied what the Bible says about investing, reading books by Austin Prior, Ron Blue, and Larry Burkett. He also completed our in-depth biblical financial study, "Financial Management God's Way."

The most important lesson George learned was that God owned everything (Psalm 24:1–2) and that he was merely a steward or manager of the money God had entrusted to him (Matthew 25:14–30). This new biblical mindset led George to diligently apply God's biblical financial principles to his life, such as contentment and the importance of debt reduction. In addition, he realized that money in and of itself is temporary, but giving generously to God's work reaps eternal rewards! As a result, over time, George experienced the joy of giving.

As George grew in his understanding of God's word concerning finances, he applied biblical principles to investing, including diversification (Ecclesiastes 11:2), not using debt to invest (Deuteronomy 28:1–12), and investing little by little over time (Proverbs 21:5). As time progressed, God blessed George's investments with above-average returns.

QUESTIONS #1
What financial deceptions did George believe during his twenties? Please provide a reference to Scripture.

TOM'S COMMENT
George believed the deception that he could obtain financial freedom by having a lot of money (John 8:31–32). In addition, he accepted the lie that "smart people use other people's money," demonstrated by his aggressive use of debt to try to substantially increase investment returns (Proverbs 22:7; 27:1; James 4:11–13).

In trying to build a large portfolio, George likely believed the financial deception that if he had more money, he would be happy. In other words, he bought into the lie that wealth and material possessions provide happiness (Ecclesiastes 5:10; John 14:26–27; Galatians 5:22–23).

QUESTION #2
What ungodly or worldly attitudes did George possess in his twenties? Please provide a reference to Scripture.

TOM'S COMMENT

- George had a strong desire to get rich quickly (Proverbs 23:4–5).
- He displayed an attitude of greed (Luke 12:15).
- He had a prideful heart since he believed he was able to build a large portfolio using his own knowledge without God's help (James 4:6–7).
- George thought he had everything figured out to make a prosperous life on his own; therefore he acted independently of God (John 15:5).

QUESTION #3
What godly attitudes and perspectives did George display in his thirties? Please provide a reference to Scripture.

TOM'S COMMENT

- George looked to God and His word for wisdom on financial matters (James 1:5). Psalm 111:10 states, "The fear of the Lord is the beginning of wisdom; all who follow his precepts have good understanding."
- He recognized that he was a steward and not an owner of the money and material things God entrusted to him (1 Chronicles 29:11–12).
- He learned contentment with respect to investment returns and likely his lifestyle (Philippians 4:11–13).
- He made debt reduction a priority (Proverbs 22:7; Romans 13:8).
- He focused on things of eternal value, not of temporal value (Matthew 6:19–21).
- He learned to give to God's work and experienced the joy of giving (2 Corinthians 8:1–8).

QUESTION #4

Suppose George had married in his late twenties before he learned God's way of managing money. What financial challenges would George and his wife likely encounter? How would these likely affect their relationship?

TOM'S COMMENT

First of all, George and his wife would not spend much time together due to George's second job. In addition, their debt would likely put pressure on both spouses and cause significant stress between them. Further, unless George's wife understood

God's financial principles, she would probably believe the same financial deceptions as George.

Each of these factors would have a detrimental effect on their marriage relationship since increasing debt increases stress between husband and wife.

QUESTION #5

What benefits would George and his wife likely enjoy after George learned and implemented biblical financial principles?

TOM'S COMMENT

Once George and his wife learned and applied God's financial principles, they would have learned contentment (Philippians 4:11–13), made debt reduction a priority (Proverbs 22:7), and developed an eternal perspective on money (Matthew 6:19–21). In addition, they would give generously (Luke 6:38) and experience God's peace (John 14:27) in their finances.

Please consider the relevance and application of the following verses with respect to George's situation. Write your thoughts below each verse.

"Do not wear yourself out to get rich; do not trust your own cleverness. Cast but a glance at riches, and they are gone, for they will surely sprout wings and fly off to the sky like an eagle" (Proverbs 23:4–5).

TOM'S COMMENT

During his twenties, George was overly focused on making a lot of money to get rich quickly. God and His word warn against this ungodly attitude.

"Keep your lives free from the love of money and be content with what you have, because God has said, 'Never will I leave you; never will I forsake you'" (Hebrews 13:5).

TOM'S COMMENT

With God's help, George needs to learn to be content with the Lord's provision.

"'God opposes the proud but shows favor to the humble.' Humble yourselves, therefore, under God's mighty hand, that he may lift you up in due time" (1 Peter 5:5–6).

TOM'S COMMENT

George was likely proud in his twenties and overconfident in his ability to quickly make a lot of money using debt. Any form of pride is contrary to God's word. The Lord desires that we humble ourselves, learn and apply His financial principles, and rely on Him for provision and guidance (John 15:5; Psalm 32:8).

"Remember this: Whoever sows sparingly will also reap sparingly, and whoever sows generously will also reap generously. Each of you should give what you have decided in your heart to give, not reluctantly or under compulsion, for God loves a cheerful giver" (2 Corinthians 9:6–7).

19. Case Study #4: "Stepping Out in Faith" and the Prosperity Gospel

Joe recently accepted Jesus Christ as his Lord and Saviour. After watching a few television evangelists, he believed that he deserved to live an extravagant lifestyle as a child of the King of kings and Lord of lords. When Joe graduated from university, he had significant student loan debt. He obtained a full-time job that paid well; however, instead of paying down his debt, he purchased a brand-new car with zero per cent financing, joined an expensive golf club, and dined out often. Basically, he "lived the high life."

By his late twenties, Joe had accumulated a lot of debt from multiple credit cards, a personal line of credit, and an expensive car loan. Nevertheless, he believed that he should be able to afford a large house since he was a "child of the King." Unfortunately, he did not have a down payment, nor had he prepared a budget or cash flow projection for this purchase.

When he went to the bank, he was approved for a substantial mortgage. This did not concern Joe as he had believed in the "prosperity gospel" teachings, which sounded good to him. Therefore, he felt assured that his faith in God's supernatural provision would enable him to live an affluent lifestyle. As a result, he "stepped out in faith" to purchase the large house and trust God for the loan payments.

Joe accumulated a large debt within three years and could not make minimum payments on his credit cards or line of credit. He also missed several mortgage payments. As a result, the auto finance company repossessed his car, and the bank foreclosed on his house, causing him to be evicted. Joe could not understand why this was happening to him! After all, he reasoned, as a child of the "Most High God," didn't he have the right to enjoy prosperity?

QUESTION #1

What financial deceptions did Joe believe? Please list them below and provide a reference to Scripture.

TOM'S COMMENT

Here are some of the financial deceptions Joe believed.

- As a Christian and child of God, Joe believed he was entitled to live an expensive lifestyle according to the "prosperity gospel." This is not true! As noted earlier, Jesus Christ, the apostle Paul, and John the Baptist all led relatively modest lives. Hebrews 13:5 states, "Keep your lives free from the love of money and be content with what you have."

- Joe believed the financial deception that it was acceptable to use debt to buy something—even without a down payment or ability to service the debt. He bought into the lie that all he had to do as a committed Christian was to *"step out in faith"* and trust God for the money to meet his financial obligations. The best example of this was when he had no down payment for a house and borrowed the maximum amount the bank would lend him for a mortgage. It does not take faith to buy something on credit! Unbelievers do this all the time. However, it takes considerable faith to trust God for the cash or a good-sized down payment on a house. (Depending on your cash flow, I recommend a minimum of 20 per cent.) In other words, do not borrow the maximum amount the bank will lend you. Create your own budget (or cash flow plan) to ensure you have a surplus each month for regular expenses and unexpected ones, which will realistically arise.

- Joe likely believed the financial deception, "If I had more money, I would be happy."
- Joe probably thought it made good sense to "buy now and pay later." This was evidenced by the fact that he had considerable debt from university, and he incurred more debt after graduation with the purchase of an expensive car and house.

QUESTION #2

Suppose Joe became open to some biblically based financial advice. What financial advice would you give him? Provide a Scripture reference for each point.

TOM'S COMMENT

- Joe needs to learn God's word on finances (see 2 Timothy 3:16–17). I would suggest that he get involved in an intensive biblical financial study, like "Financial Management God's Way". This is available at no cost on our website, www.coplandfinancialministries.org. I also offer Zoom and in-class versions of this study during the year.
- Joe needs to understand that God discourages debt and warns of the dangers of debt (see Proverbs 22:7). Throughout the Bible, when God met needs, He did so with no debt! (Deuteronomy 28:11–12). Therefore, for most purchases (except for a house or first-time automobile purchase), Joe should truly "step out in faith" and trust

God to provide the cash if it is God's will for him to buy something (see Proverbs 3:5–6).

- Joe needs to learn that the prosperity gospel is *not* consistent with Scripture. Yes, God can bless some people financially, as He did with Abraham, Solomon, David, and Job, but that's not always the case. A good example is the apostle Paul, who wrote more than half the New Testament but had very little. In fact, Paul was imprisoned when he wrote a number of his epistles.
- Joe needs to develop and implement a budget to ensure he spends less than he earns so he can pay off his debt and save for future needs, like a down payment on a house (see Luke 14:28–30).
- Joe must learn contentment and live within his means as provided by the Lord (see Philippians 4:1–13).

20. Personal Testimony and Summary of Chapter V on Financial Deceptions

When I accepted Jesus Christ as my Lord and Saviour on April 12, 1981, I had a lot of debt. I had not followed biblical financial principles because I didn't know what they were. Shortly thereafter, I obtained a number of resources authored by Larry Burkett, who was a great teacher of God's word on finances. As I listened to his teaching many times over the next year, I was amazed that the Bible contained so much wisdom and practical advice on finances. I meditated upon a number of key Scriptures. God spoke to me through His word (Hebrews 4:12) and His Spirit (John 10:27), and God changed the way I thought about and hence the way I managed money.

In 1982, in the middle of a recession when interest rates were 18 to 20 per cent, God directed me to start my own accounting practice. I had almost no clients. But over the next three years, as I learned and implemented biblical financial principles, including giving 10 per cent to the Lord's work, God did amazing things and provided me with many clients, including some very large ones who would normally not use a sole practitioner. And praise God, within three years I was totally debt-free—no mortgage and no debt whatsoever! That was 1985, and I've never borrowed any money since then.

The truth is that God's word contains incredible wisdom on finances! I quickly realized that most people believed many "financial deceptions" from the world and Satan. Consequently, they have not followed God's biblical financial principles and have later suffered the consequences.

After four decades of teaching God's word on finances, I can confidently say that the way people manage money has only worsened. Today, many consistently violate God's financial principles and carry substantial debt. Sadly, most Christians, and people in general, have limited knowledge of what the Bible says on finances, so they believe in false concepts or "financial deceptions." As a result, they manage money the wrong way—the world's way rather than God's way.

However, there is a straightforward solution! First, people need to change how they think about finances by studying and meditating on God's word (Romans 12:2; Joshua 1:8). This way, they will gain the "mind of Christ" and learn to manage money according to biblical principles. Furthermore, as a follower of Jesus, it's essential not just to be a "hearer of the word" but also a "doer of the word" (James 1:22). In other words, it is vital not only to study God's word but also to apply it consistently to how people manage the money He has entrusted to them.

Over the years, I have provided biblically based financial advice to thousands of people, and I have complete confidence in the authority of God's word. I believe that if people study and apply God's word on finances, and if they learn to distinguish between a "financial deception" and God's truth, they will be far better off financially (John 8:32).

In what ways will they be better off? In general, those who follow biblical financial principles will have little or no debt, enough savings for their retirement and their children's education, and an emergency fund. In addition, they will enjoy a more fulfilling life without the burden of debt and financial hardship. Another benefit is that disciples of Jesus will be able to give generously to God's work to build His kingdom on earth and build up treasures in heaven (Matthew 16:27)!

Overall, people will experience God's peace in their finances, which impacts every area of life and beyond.

In John 14:27, Jesus said, "Peace I leave with you; my peace I give you. I do not give to you as the world gives. Do not let your hearts be troubled and do not be afraid."

To learn more about God's word on finances, be sure to access our resources at www.coplandfinancialministries.org, most of which are free.

VI

DISCERNING GOD'S WILL THROUGH YOUR RELATIONSHIP WITH CHRIST

In some circumstances, God's word provides very specific guidance regarding finances. For example, in Exodus 20:17, God commanded his people, "You shall *not covet your neighbor's house*. You shall not covet your neighbor's wife, or his male or female servant, his ox or donkey, *or anything that belongs to your neighbor*" (emphasis added).

However, the Bible does not always provide specific direction when an individual or couple face a financial decision. However, it does present principles or guidelines that God wants us to follow. Within those guidelines there can be several options. And it is only through a personal relationship with Jesus Christ that you can discover God's specific will for your life.

Be assured that God has promised to direct us. In Psalm 32:8, God said, "I will instruct you and teach you in the way you should go; I will counsel you with my loving eye on you."

Let's consider a Christian couple who manages money according to biblical principles. They develop and implement a budget, have godly motives, spend wisely, and are content with God's provision. In essence, they are good stewards of the money God has entrusted to them.

Whenever they quiet themselves before the Lord in prayer, they sense God leading them to purchase a house. They now seek God's wisdom and specific direction on how to proceed.

Many questions arise: Do they require a four-bedroom house, or will a three-bedroom house meet their needs? Is it necessary to buy a house with a two-car garage, or could a one-car garage suffice? In what price range should they buy a house? Most importantly, what can they comfortably afford, and what is the maximum amount they should borrow?

As they contemplate, they realize that there are several options that are all within God's financial principles. To determine God's specific will for this critical financial decision, I suggest the following.

- Pray and ask God for His wisdom (James 1:5) and His specific direction (Psalm 32:8) regarding this important decision.
- Prayerfully read God's word and ask God, through His Holy Spirit, to highlight specific verses related to their decision. God's word can reveal His will to them. Psalm 119:105 says, "Your word is a lamp for my feet, a light on my path."
- Ask God to provide His peace or lack of peace concerning a potential decision. When we follow God's will, we will experience His peace. In John 14:27, Jesus gave this promise: "Peace I leave with you; my peace I give you. I do not give to you as the world gives. Do not let your hearts be troubled and do not be afraid."
- In prayer, "Be still before the LORD and wait patiently for him" (Psalm 37:7). Ask the Holy Spirit of God to speak to their hearts and minds. In John 10:27, Jesus said, "My sheep listen to my voice; I know them, and they follow me." Although God can speak to you audibly as he did with Moses, it is more likely he will speak to you through His word (Hebrews 4:12), through a godly financial adviser (1 Corinthians 2:14–15), and by His Spirit.
- Obtain biblical counsel from at least two godly financial advisers (Psalm 1:1–3) who will not benefit financially from whatever you plan to purchase.

- Ask God to show you how and where He is working. Jesus revealed a remarkable truth in John 5:19 when he said: "Very truly I tell you, the Son can do nothing by himself; he can do only what he sees his Father doing, because whatever the Father does the Son also does."
- And finally, ask God to provide his direction through specific circumstances—to open and close the right doors. Like Gideon, who set out a "fleece" to seek God's direction and confirmation (Judges 6:37–40). However, be cautious to discern the Lord's will accurately when taking on debt. The availability of credit may not be from God, but a temptation from Satan to lure you into taking on too much debt.

For financial decisions involving several options, there is absolutely no substitute for spending considerable quality time in prayer seeking God's wisdom and specific direction (Psalm 25:12). This should include the seven steps just outlined.

It is essential to have a personal relationship with Jesus Christ to discern with accuracy God's leading in every area of your life, including your financial decisions.

The following outlines how you can develop a personal relationship with Jesus Christ.

1. God Loves You, and He Desires a Personal Relationship with You

In John 10:3–4, Jesus, the Son of God, said:

The gatekeeper [God the Father] opens the gate for him [Jesus Christ], and the sheep [His followers, Christians] listen to his voice. He [Jesus Christ] calls his own sheep by name and leads them out. When he has brought out all his own, he goes on ahead of them, and his sheep follow him because they know his voice.

Further, in John 10:14–15, Jesus said: "I am the good shepherd; I know my sheep and my sheep know me—just as the Father knows me and I know the Father—and I lay down my life for the sheep."

It is important for you to understand that God loves you unconditionally, and He longs to have a personal relationship with you. However, sin stands in the way.

2. Our Sin Separates Us from God

Romans 3:23 says, "All have sinned and fall short of the glory of God," and Romans 6:23 states, "The wages of sin is death, but the gift of God is eternal life in Christ Jesus our Lord."

And Isaiah 59:2 makes it clear: "Your iniquities have separated you from your God; your sins have hidden his face from you, so that he will not hear."

Please think about this diagram, which shows that man is on one side and God is on the other side. A deep chasm separates sinful people and a Holy God.

Our sin results in separation from God.

MAN
(Sinful)

GOD
(Holy)

3. Many Seek God the Wrong Way

It is written in Proverbs 14:12, "There is a way that appears to be right, but in the end it leads to death." Ephesians 2:8–9 clearly states that all people are entirely dependent on the Lord Jesus Christ for eternal salvation: "It is by grace you have been saved, through faith—and this is not from yourselves, it is the gift of God—not by works, so that no one can boast."

In other words, *we cannot earn our way to heaven* through good works, religion, philosophy, morality, or any other means, as illustrated here diagrammatically:

None of our efforts can bridge this gap.
There is only one remedy for this problem
of separation from God...

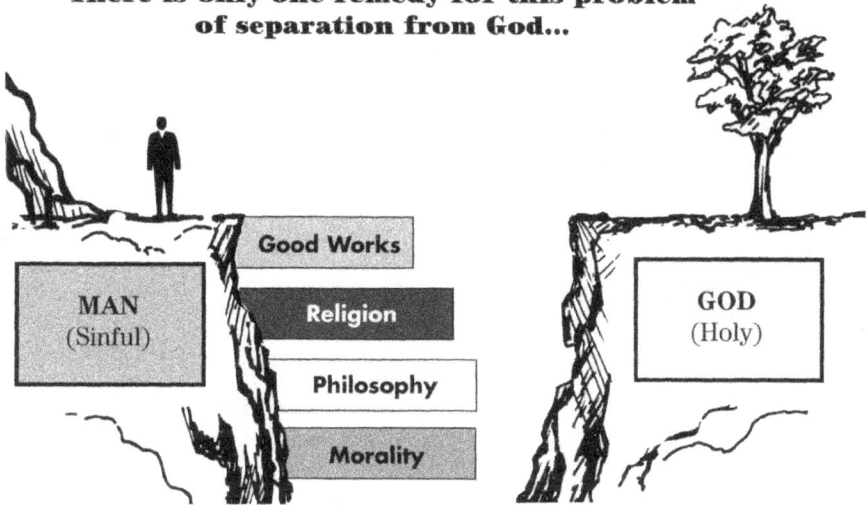

MAN
(Sinful)

Good Works

Religion

Philosophy

Morality

GOD
(Holy)

4. God Provides the Only Solution to Sin—His Son, Jesus Christ

In John 14:6, Jesus answered, "I am the way and the truth and the life. No one comes to the Father except through me."

The words of Romans 5:8 give us hope: "God demonstrates his own love for us in this: While we were still sinners, Christ died for us."

In other words, Jesus Christ provided the only solution by his death on the cross for the forgiveness of our sins.

**God has provided the only solution.
We must make the choice...**

5. Are You Willing to Do the Following?

1. The first step to reconciliation with God is to admit that you are a sinner who has sinned against God. Romans 3:23 tells us, "For all have sinned and fall short of the glory of God."

2. Considering this truth, you must turn away from your sins, follow God, and obey him (Deuteronomy 28:1–12; Romans 10:9–10).

3. Believe that Jesus Christ died to forgive you of your sins, then open your heart to accept Him as your personal Lord and Saviour. John 3:16 says, "For God so loved the world that he gave his one and only Son, that whoever believes in him shall not perish but have eternal life."

4. Prayerfully call upon Jesus Christ to enter your heart and to take control of your life through the supernatural work of the Holy Spirit. In Revelation 3:20, Jesus provides you with this invitation when He says, "Here I am! I stand at the door and knock. If anyone hears my voice and opens the door, I will come in and eat with that person, and they with me." The "door" represents a person's heart.

Please understand that all I have done is cite some key Scriptures of the Bible. If you sense the desire to put your faith and trust in Jesus Christ, then the Holy Spirit of God is knocking at the door of your heart. Allow God's Spirit to enter your heart and give you His wisdom and guidance.

To accomplish this, I recommend you pray the following prayer to the Lord of the universe:

Dear Father God, I know I am a sinner and that I need Your forgiveness. I believe that Your Son, Jesus Christ, died for my sins. I am willing to turn from my sins. I now invite Jesus Christ to come into my heart and my life as my personal Lord and Saviour. I am willing, by God's strength, to follow and obey Jesus Christ as the Lord of my life.

6. If You Prayed This Prayer from Your Heart, Here Are Some Promises from God

"Everyone who calls on the name of the Lord will be saved" (Romans 10:13). Saved from what? In 2 Thessalonians 1:8–9, God's position is clear:

He will punish those who do not know God and do not obey the gospel of our Lord Jesus. They will be punished with everlasting destruction and shut out from the presence of the Lord and from the glory of his might.

In other words, if you reject Jesus Christ as your Lord and Saviour, you will suffer eternal separation from God. The Bible refers to this as "hell," also known as "Hades" in Greek. Whatever name you ascribe to it, such a place is based on biblical truth. My intention is not to be mean, but rather to tell you the truth for your eternal benefit. Therefore, I strongly encourage you to accept Jesus Christ as your personal Lord and Saviour today.

If you committed your life to the Lord, here's another promise from God, as stated in John 1:12–13:

To all who did receive him, to those who believed in his name, he gave the right to become children of God—children born not of natural descent, nor of human decision or a husband's will, but born of God.

If you sincerely prayed this prayer or a similar prayer, and accepted Jesus Christ as your personal Lord and Saviour, then you are a child of God. You are now privileged to enjoy a personal relationship with the Lord of the universe!

If this is the first time you've accepted Jesus Christ as your Lord and Saviour, please visit www.coplandfinancialministries.org, and send me an email so that I can share some helpful literature with you and encourage you in your walk with the Lord!

VII
CONCLUSION AND RECOMMENDED FOLLOW-UP

This is a summary of *Biblical Principles to Deal with Inflation, Higher Interest, and Eliminating Debt,* and recommended follow-up.

1. Chapter I: God's Wisdom on Debt and the Importance of Saving

God's word, the Bible, has incredible wisdom to share concerning money management. Unfortunately, most people have limited knowledge of what the Bible says about finances. Therefore, they fail to follow biblical financial principles only to suffer the consequences later.

According to Psalm 37:21, it is not a sin to borrow money, but it is a sin to borrow and not repay. And in Proverbs 22:7, God discourages debt and warns us of the dangers of debt. In fact, throughout Scripture, God met needs with no debt. For example, Deuteronomy 28:1–12 demonstrates how God blessed His people in every area of their lives, including their finances, meeting their needs supernaturally—without any debt!

Another important financial principle is that God admonishes us to plan and save for future needs. In Proverbs 21:5, we learn that "the plans of the diligent lead to profit as surely as haste leads to poverty." In other words, disciplined saving along the way can avoid future debt and hardship.

Further, Proverbs 21:20 states, "The wise man saves for the future, but the foolish man spends whatever he gets" (TBL).

On the other hand, the wisdom of the world today is to buy now, pay later, and use credit liberally. Today, you can purchase almost anything on credit. Easy credit creates an incredible temptation for people to spend more than they earn. Consequently, the majority of people carry a lot of debt. Unexpected events in their lives, such as an illness or job loss, could leave them in serious financial trouble—they could lose their car or home or be forced into bankruptcy.

2. Chapter II: How to Get Out of Debt

In chapter II, I provided seven suggested steps on how you can reduce your debt with the goal of becoming totally debt-free.

Here's a summary of those seven steps.

1. Pray and ask God for His wisdom and specific direction (James 1:5).
2. Study and meditate on God's word related to finances (Joshua 1:8). and implement God's financial principles in your life (James 1:22).
3. Evaluate your present financial position—assets, liabilities, revenues, and expenses (Proverbs 27:23).
4. Develop and implement a budget (Luke 14:28–30).
5. Learn to be content with God's provision (Philippians 4:11–13).
6. With your surplus cash, pay off the most expensive debt and any non-deductible debt first (Proverbs 22:7).
7. Depend on God, follow through, and persevere until you are debt-free. Jesus said, "My grace is sufficient for you, for my power is made perfect in weakness" (2 Corinthians 12:9).

I assure you that God's best is that you have no debt whatsoever, and if you make that a priority, you will be glad you did!

3. Chapter III: How to Develop and Implement a Budget

In order to get out of debt and to manage your monthly cash flow well, it is essential to track your expenses so you know your "financial facts" rather than guessing. Further, you need to develop and implement a budget—if you prefer, you can call it a spending plan or cash flow plan, as they are basically the same thing.

Many people regard budgeting in a negative light for various reasons. Unfortunately, when people do not adhere to a budget or God's financial principles, they will likely spend more than they earn, accumulate debt, and end up with a host of financial problems at a future date.

4. Chapter IV: Questions to Consider Before Borrowing and Co-Signing

The following list summarizes the questions you should consider before you borrow a significant amount of money.

1. Do you have a plan (Proverbs 21:5), such as a budget, to ensure you can comfortably afford the loan payments?
2. Do you understand it is your responsibility to repay the entire loan (Psalm 37:21) and to make the payments on time? After all, what kind of "light in a world of darkness" is a Christian who does not pay their debts on time (Matthew 5:16)?
3. Have you prayed for a reasonable amount of time and given God an opportunity to provide the funds in a way that glorifies Him? As Isaiah 64:4 indicates, God acts on behalf of those who wait for Him.
4. Have you given God the opportunity to provide what you need at a lower cost or perhaps an alternative? (Psalm 37:7).

5. Have you considered that God simply may not want you to have what you are asking for? At times, it is God's best for us to forgo the purchase of a particular material item (Matthew 16:24–25).

6. Is the item you plan to purchase a necessity? Can you manage without it? God has promised to meet our needs but not necessarily our wants and desires (Matthew 6:31–33).

7. Have you and your spouse, if you're married, prayed sincerely for God's guidance? Do you have God's peace about this potential expense (Genesis 2:24; John 14:26–27)?

8. Finally, most importantly, have you spent sufficient time in prayer with the Lord, seeking His specific direction before making any significant financial decisions? One of my favorite Scriptures is Isaiah 48:17, "I am the LORD your God, who teaches you what is best for you, who directs you in the way you should go."

Most people are unaware that God's word strongly advises against co-signing. Proverbs 11:15 says, "It's a dangerous thing to guarantee payment for someone's debts. Don't do it!" (CEV). This is a principle, not a law. It is not a sin to co-sign, but God warns of the dangers of doing so.

Remember, if you co-sign a loan, you may have to pay a debt you don't owe. Second, if you co-sign and have to pay the loan because the borrower defaults, your relationship with the borrower may become strained. This is because a co-signer often feels resentful that they had to pay a debt that was not theirs, and the borrower who did not meet its financial obligations often feels guilty.

If someone asks you to co-sign for them, usually a family member or close friend, and they have a genuine need, consider giving them the money if you can. Alternatively, if you choose to lend money, it is best to lend expecting nothing in return. That way, if the borrower defaults, the relationship between the two parties remains intact.

5. Chapter V: Financial Deceptions

We are bombarded with many false concepts of finance in our world today. I call these "financial deceptions." A financial deception is a belief that appears to be correct, but it is contrary to God's word.

If you believe and follow these financial deceptions, you will come into financial bondage and face major financial problems in due course.

I've summarized the financial deceptions.

Deception #1: It's Okay to Live Paycheque-to-Paycheque
Deception #2: You Should Gain Financial Freedom Quickly
Deception #3: Debt Restructuring Solves Financial Issues
Deception #4: More Money Brings Happiness
Deception #5: "Buy Now and Pay Later" Makes Sense
Deception #6: Smart People Use Other People's Money
Deception #7: A Lot of Money Equals Financial Freedom
Deception #8: Bankruptcy Solves Financial Problems
Deception #9: Faith-Filled Christians Will Enjoy Prosperity
Deception #10: "Step Out in Faith" and Trust God for the
Payments

6. Chapter VI: Discerning God's Will Through Your Relationship with Christ

Generally, the Bible provides us with financial guidelines. However, there can be several options. To determine God's specific will for any important financial decision, I suggest the following.

1. Pray and ask God for His wisdom (James 1:5) and His specific direction (Psalm 32:8) regarding this important decision.
2. Prayerfully read God's word, and ask God, through His Holy Spirit, to highlight specific related verses to direct you (Psalms 119:105).
3. Ask God to provide His peace or lack of peace concerning a potential decision (John 14:27).
4. In prayer, "Be still before the LORD" (Psalm 37:7). Ask God to speak to your heart and mind (John 10:27) or through His word (Hebrews 4:12).
5. Obtain biblical counsel from at least two godly financial advisers (Psalm 1:1–3) who will not benefit financially from whatever you plan to purchase.
6. Ask God to show you how and where He is working (John 5:19–20).
7. And finally, ask God to provide His direction through specific circumstances—to open and close the right doors. However, be cautious: the availability of credit may not be from God, but a temptation from Satan to lure you into taking on too much debt.

For financial decisions involving several options, there is absolutely no substitute for spending considerable quality time in prayer seeking God's wisdom and specific direction (Psalm 25:12). This should include the seven steps just outlined. And before you move ahead, be sure to obtain God's peace (John 14:27) regarding the proposed financial decision.

7. Chapter VII: Conclusion and Recommended Follow-Up

As a servant of the Lord Jesus Christ, the Lord has appointed me to teach His word on finances. Since 1982, it has been a privilege to help thousands reduce their debt, with many becoming completely debt-free. No one has ever regretted having less debt or no debt. As a result, many people have praised God for the wisdom of His word, and their financial stress was substantially reduced or eliminated entirely.

I cannot stress enough that there is no substitute for studying and meditating on God's word concerning your finances. Psalm 119:105 states, "Your word is a lamp for my feet, a light on my path." Most of us have believed lies and deceptions from the world. It takes time and hard work to allow God, through His word (Hebrews 4:12) and his Spirit (John 10:27), to change the way we think about money and material things. Once you adopt a godly perspective, instead of a worldly perspective, you will manage money God's way. Again, the battle is for your mind.

In Romans 12:2, the apostle Paul admonishes us, "Do not conform to the pattern of this world, but be transformed by the renewing of your mind. Then you will be able to test and approve what God's will is—his good, pleasing and perfect will." And how do we renew our minds? Joshua 1:8 gives the answer, "Keep this Book of the Law always on your lips; meditate on it day and night, so that you may be careful to do everything written in it. Then you will be prosperous and successful."

To learn more about God's word on finances and to ensure you are implementing the biblical financial principles in managing the money God has entrusted to you, I encourage you to go to our website, www.coplandfinancialministries.org, and access our many resources, most of which are free.

My first recommendation is for you to take part in our in-depth biblical financial study, "Financial Management God's Way." This eleven-week study requires two hours of class time per week and about three hours of homework per week. Through this study, we have seen the most dramatic and permanent changes in the way people think about and manage money. You can join one of our Zoom small groups or access the online version on your own, with your spouse, or your children. Further, many small group leaders have found that using this video series makes it easy to lead a group financial study. I would encourage you to do that in your own local church or even on your own with a group of friends. If you need any help, please contact us.

Besides the "Financial Management God's Way" series, here is an overview of the other resources available on our website:

- Discerning God's Will in Managing Money: Advanced workshop with eight half-hour videos.
- Debt Reduction God's Way: CD/DVD workshop and online series.
- God's Financial Wisdom for Business: CD and online series.
- Debt Reduction God's Way for Business: CD and online series.
- Biblically Based Estate Planning: Audio and online series.
- Tom's Top Financial Moments: Single CD with 70 "Financial Moments."
- Copland Budgeting System: Free downloadable Excel-based forms.
- Financial Moments Podcast: Online video and audio.
- Half-hour videos on many financial topics.
- Articles and other resources.
- Financial Moments email list. Be sure to register for this on our website so you can receive a Financial Moment each week and be advised of upcoming workshops either in person or by Zoom.

• Biblically based financial coaching, which is provided on a ministry basis at no charge. Please go to our website and send us an email.

8. Tom's Final Comments

This book aims to help people get their finances in order and, in particular, to get out of debt. As of writing this book in the spring of 2022, the debt loads in Canada, the United States, and around the globe are at record highs—at the personal, corporate, and government levels. In addition, until early 2022, we have enjoyed low interest rates for many years; this has recently changed as central banks worldwide are increasing interest rates to control inflation.

I don't presume to know the future (James 4:13–15), as only God knows the future (Isaiah 46:10). However, from 45 years of experience in the financial sector, I do know this: if individuals, couples, or business owners learn and apply God's financial principles as outlined in the Bible, they will reduce their debt, increase their monthly cash flow, and develop savings for unexpected and future expenses.

As a side benefit, those who follow and implement biblical financial principles will experience God's peace in the area of their finances. In John 14:27, Jesus said, "Peace I leave with you, my peace I give you. I do not give to you as the world gives. Do not let your hearts be troubled and do not be afraid."

Visit www.coplandfinanicalministries.org to access our many resources and ensure you learn more about God's word on finances—that you are a "doer of the word and not just a hearer of the word" (James 1:22). Alternatively, follow us on Facebook, Instagram, Twitter, or under Bible finance. If you have questions or would like some financial coaching, you can contact me at tcopland@zing-net.ca.

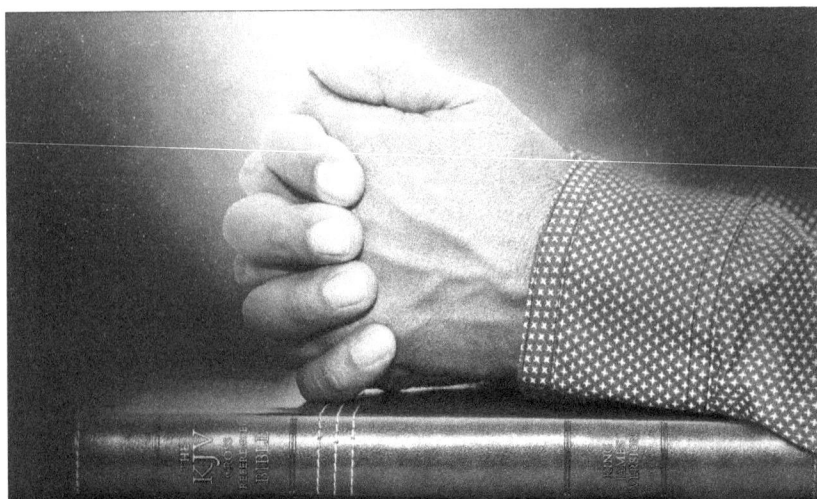

FINANCIAL MOMENTS

WITH TOM COPLAND
(Chartered Professional Accountant)

*Biblical Principles that Will
Transform How You Manage Money*

CASTLE QUAY BOOKS

www.ingramcontent.com/pod-product-compliance
Lightning Source LLC
Chambersburg PA
CBHW031242090426
42742CB00007B/277